The Penguin Book of Modern African Poetry

Gerald Moore was born in London in 1924. After serving in the Navy during the war he read English at Emmanuel College, Cambridge. Apart from ten years in the School of African and Asian Studies at Sussex, he has taught at universities in various parts of Africa and in Hong Kong. He has also been Visiting Professor at UCLA, the University of Wisconsin (Madison), the University of Ghana and the University of Ife. He now lives in Italy with his wife and younger son.

His publications include *The Chosen Tongue: English Writing in the Tropical World* (1969), *Wole Soyinka* (1978), *Twelve African Writers* (1984) and three earlier editions of the present anthology. He has also published translations of Mongo Beti, Henri Lopes, Tchicaya U Tam'si and J.-B. Tati-Loutard.

Ulli Beier was born in Germany in 1922. From 1950 to 1971 he taught literature and creative writing at the universities of Ibadan (Nigeria) and Papua New Guinea. During the period 1971 to 1978 he was director of research institutes in Nigeria and New Guinea. In 1981 he founded and directed IWALEWA Haus, a centre for contemporary art, music and literature from the Third World. Ulli Beier has lived in Sydney as a freelance writer since 1996.

His publications include *Introduction to African Literature* (1964); *Contemporary Art in Africa* (1968); *Yoruba Poetry* (1970), *Thirty Years of Oshogbo Art* (1991); and *Yoruba – das Überleben einer Kultur* (1991). He founded and edited five literary and cultural magazines, including *Black Orpheus – A Journal of African and Afro-American Literature* (1957–67).

The Penguin Book of **Modern African Poetry**

Edited by GERALD MOORE *and* ULLI BEIER

PENGUIN BOOKS

PENGUIN BOOKS

Published by the Penguin Group
Penguin Books Ltd, 27 Wrights Lane, London w8 5tz, England
Penguin Putnam Inc., 375 Hudson Street, New York, New York 10014, USA
Penguin Books Australia Ltd, Ringwood, Victoria, Australia
Penguin Books Canada Ltd, 10 Alcorn Avenue, Toronto, Ontario, Canada m4v 3b2
Penguin Books (NZ) Ltd, 182–190 Wairau Road, Auckland 10, New Zealand

Penguin Books Ltd, Registered Offices: Harmondsworth, Middlesex, England

Modern Poetry from Africa first published 1963
Second edition published 1968
Third edition published as *The Penguin Book of Modern African Poetry* 1984
Fourth edition first published 1998
10 9 8 7 6 5 4 3 2

This collection copyright © Gerald Moore and Ulli Beier, 1963, 1968, 1984, 1998
Introduction copyright © Gerald Moore, 1998
All rights reserved
The Acknowledgements on pages 435–437 constitute an extension of this copyright page

The moral right of the editors has been asserted

Set in Monotype Garamond and Monotype Gill Sans
Typeset by Rowland Phototypesetting Ltd, Bury St Edmunds, Suffolk
Printed in England by Clays Ltd, St Ives plc

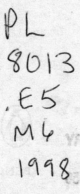

Contents

Namibia

Nigeria

Introduction

'Come and hope and dream with me' sang Mongane Wally Serote in 1994, the year of Nelson Mandela's election as President of South Africa. It will serve quite well as a superscription for this new edition. Not that all breathes hope therein, or in the Africa that gave it birth. But that election, the relatively peaceful transfer of power from a dominant minority to a majority, has to be the outstanding political event of Africa in the nineties. Outstanding not only because so long-awaited, but because it was unprecedented in history and ran counter to many sober predictions of bloody and desperate conflict. As had happened before in Kenya and Zimbabwe, it was the very man most demonized by the former masters who won most credit in the manner of the transfer. Serote's hailing of the event in his long poem *Come and Hope with Me*, written soon after his own return from prolonged exile, forms a matching peak in the poetry of the same epoch, for it was a poem which had been as long agathering within his work as the final struggle for emancipation which began at Sharpeville in 1960. The note it strikes is a good one on which to open, because it reminds us that not all has been gloom and retrogression in the continent over the past dozen years, however much the daily bulletins might tempt us to think so. This edition garners many new poems and many new poets from the same period, to amplify its survey of Africa's abundant creativity, her refusal to abandon those human values so long associated with her name. But it is sobering to remember how many of these same poets have suffered imprisonment, banning, exile and even death in these years; how many African countries have been plunged into civil war or military dictatorship. Poets have been and still remain in the firing line. Nor could it be otherwise, for the alternative of averting their gaze from Africa's unfolding drama simply does not exist for them. Perhaps only Russian poets, in this century, have been so embattled, so frequently muzzled by all the devices of power. In the words of another poet collected here, Mvula ya Nangolo of Namibia, 'How far is Robben Island from a black child at play?'

For it is not left to the writers to insist upon their relevance. The authorities have been just as keen to detect the intermeshing of poetry and politics, even where it is not present. As Terry Eagleton has recently written in another connection, 'Culture is integral to colonial power . . . Reading the world in terms of power is a familiar habit of the colonial subject.'[1] What was true of the colonial situation is no less true today, for the culture vacuum created by the withdrawal or abdication from power of dominant groups, the former arbiters of 'culture', cries to be filled, and poetry has been in the vanguard of that process.

Thus, while Serote rejoices in the emergence of his 'rainbow republic', Don Mattera reminds us from the streets of Johannesburg that 'If their lies are to survive/ The poet must die.' That poem, it is true, was written during the heyday of apartheid, but it would be naïve to assume that the honeymoon in the new South Africa can last for ever. The poet, by the very nature of his art, is forever skirting danger. In these pages, Jack Mapanje of Malawi guides us through the anguish of his brutal, inexplicable imprisonment and the numbing astonishment of his equally arbitrary release ('Your Tears Still Burn at My Handcuffs'). To understand the context of Mapanje's prison poems we must understand the peculiar dilemma of the political prisoner, held without charge or trial for as long as his masters see fit. Such prisoners are frequently denied all visits, all correspondence, all gifts, all communication with the outside world. Even books, pen and paper are often refused, and solitary confinement is the likely reward of any protest. All the props that might keep the normal long-term prisoner going, such as regular visits, letters, campaigns in the courts and in the media, hopes of reprieve or parole, even simply crossing off the days until release, are denied to 'politicals'. He or she has become an Orwellian 'non-person', whose very existence the authorities blandly refuse to confirm, let alone the location or reason of their confinement.

Mapanje's imprisonment, like that of many other poets included here, came like a bolt from the blue, touched off apparently by the republication of his successful first volume, *Of Chameleons and Gods*. Apart from poking a little gentle fun at the official ban on mini-skirts, there seemed little in that book at which even the censors could take offence. It is yet another proof that to many official minds the mere activity of poetry is suspect. His release three and a half years later was equally arbitrary. Certainly, international pressure seems to have had little to do with it, since that pressure had continued ever since his arrest. Apparently the dictator had woken up in a good mood. Had it been a bad one, Mapanje could just as easily have been fed to the crocodiles, like many others before him. The pain of his mother's recent death, after her long, hopeless vigil, did much to mitigate the joy of that release: 'You gave up too early, mother: two/ More months and I'd have told you the story . . .' He had to perform for himself the rituals belonging to a mother's welcome.

Meanwhile, Mapanje's fellow Malawian Frank Chipasula counts the cost of his long exile and grieves for his country from afar ('A Love Poem for My Country'). His grief bursts out in a frightful image: 'Your streets are littered with handcuffed men/ And the drums are thuds of the warders' spiked boots'. Thus Malawi's two major poets were compelled to witness tyranny from either end of the spectrum: from those of maximum distance and maximum intimacy. Their poems measure the meaning of each kind of deprivation. The Malawi Literary Festival, held in July 1996, provided a good occasion to count the blessings of the anguished continent. Its southern half, for so long the prey of civil war, cross-border raids and kidnappings, oppressive dictatorship and white minority rule, is enjoying an era of peace, freedom of movement and unprecedented freedom of expression. The worst dramas seem now to be unfolding further north. Mapanje's arbitrary imprisonment can be matched with that of Maina wa Kinyatti, held for six years in conditions of which his poems offer only a glimpse. All this in Kenya, often the darling of the Western press and the tourists, where Micere Githae Mugo also suffered long imprisonment. When the shutters open in one corner of the continent, they are all too likely to slam down in another.

Syl Cheney-Coker, on the other side of Africa, sings of the brotherhood of man, but has to witness Sierra Leone's slide from chronic military dictatorship to civil war, spreading like a disease from neighbouring Liberia. Further south, in Angola, Mawete Makisosila and

Makuzayi Massaki lament the tragic irony of an African liberation movement (the MPLA) that massacres thousands of its own supporters for being too 'indigenous', too African, not sufficiently fluent in the language of their former masters ('Indelible Traces'). What might have looked like a peculiar strength of the Angolan liberation movement, the presence within it of many of the relatively privileged mulattos, could also prove to be its weakness. Rather like the South American creole before him, the mulatto may be foremost in attacking the metropolitan power, but backmost in recognizing the real indigenous forces which threaten his privileges.

So Africa sings in her chains, as well as in the act of breaking them; for chains she still bears. Not only the familiar ones of poverty and oppression, but those newly imposed by the IMF, with its insistence on cuts in health and education services, which mortgage the future as well as the present. And all this to the background of an international community that veers between blundering interference and cynical indifference; between using helicopter gunships to hunt down a single man and turning its back on genocide. Since 1984, when the third edition of this anthology appeared, South Africa has joined Namibia in freedom; the long-running civil wars in Mozambique, Angola and Ethiopia/Eritrea (all involving external players) have drawn to a close; but there is no end in sight in the Sudan or Somalia, Liberia or Algeria, Rwanda or Burundi. While some countries struggle to rebuild after decades of war, others plumb new depths in civil anarchy and ethnic slaughter. And what of the curtain of repression that has dropped upon the creative variety and abundance of Nigeria? The body of Ken Saro-Wiwa still swings in the imagination of the world.

There is, then, many a cry of pain in these pages; much that echoes Augustinho Neto's forty-year-old lament for 'The Grieved Lands of Africa'. But there is also the mischievous humour of Kojo Laing or Femi Fatoba, two poets included for the first time. To set against their masculine banter, we have the concentrated passion of Ifi Amadiume's 'Bitter' or Gwendoline Konie's 'In the Fist of Your Hatred', both written from the receiving end of male arrogance or indifference. The whole range of mood and expression is certainly much broader than in earlier editions, extending from the elegant wit of recent poems by Niyi Osundare and Funso Aiyejina to the melodic threnodies of Ben Okri for his 'squandered nation'; all three of these poets being from Nigeria's younger generation.

The voices of Africa's many women poets also claim a larger place than before. Here acknowledgements are due to Stella and Frank Chipasula for their valuable anthology of women's poetry, and apologies to one of the pioneers among them, Alda do Espirito Santo of São Tomé, who was inadvertently 'unsexed' in earlier editions of this anthology. The explanation, though certainly not the excuse, is that the error was copied from an earlier anthology prepared by the late Janheinz Jahn. We are now glad to welcome her to her proper place as one of the foremost voices among Africa's women. Speaking of those voices, many of their poems are written as if from *within* scenes of intimate domestic oppression, like the Konie poem already cited, or Micere Mugo's 'Wife of the Husband'. The poets remind us that for many women there is no other world in which to seek redress. Their voices certainly form a powerful corrective to any earlier imbalance between the sexes. But the women are also done ample justice by Femi Fatoba himself, in the closing stanza of his poem:

> The woman
> Who wants to be my wife
> Inherited Ifa's tongue;
> We shall sleep on
> A chest of riddles and proverbs.

And Jack Mapanje does not forget to revisit the cheerful girls of Smiller's Bar, who illuminated his first collection.

All the new poems here, however, are not confined to the worlds and doings of men and women. Musaemura Zimunya's intense realization of the tarantula is only one of several precise animal studies in his first collection, *Kingfisher, Jikinya and Other Poems*. Tati-Loutard's prolific output in recent years has added much to Africa's rich marine poetry. The seascape that has dominated his imagination ever since his *Poèmes de la mer* in 1968 continues to challenge him by its difference and indifference. In his 'Letter to Edouard Maunick', he salutes a fellow marine poet, but this one an islander, from the far side of Africa.

Altogether this edition presents the work of ninety-nine poets, thirty-one of whom are presented for the first time. Their dates of birth span the first sixty years of the century and their countries of origin number twenty-seven, with Namibia, Zambia and Zimbabwe among the new additions. The poets range from acknowledged masters like L. S. Senghor, Augustinho Neto, Tchicaya U Tam'si, Okot p'Bitek and Christopher Okigbo to poets who are still at the beginning of their development. Among the masters, death or old age has closed the activity of many. Since 1984, African poetry has registered the loss of Tchicaya U Tam'si, one of the most powerful and distinctive voices of his generation. Of the poets now included, thirteen are women and thirty-seven have been translated from languages other than English. No malice is intended towards any country or poet excluded. Space imposes its own disciplines and has to be used to reflect the taste of the editor. Other editors may make other choices from the vast field now available. But to reflect one's own taste is not an act of self-indulgence; it is the essence of the anthologist's art.

What can be said in summary of such wealth and variety as can be found in these pages? Poetry, always foremost of the arts in traditional Africa, has continued to compete for primacy against the newer forms of prose fiction and theatre drama. Even the African novelists (unlike their Western equivalents) often fill their narratives with songs, myths and dreams. As for the sources of expression, some of the poems here come straight from the front line, like those of Mvula wa Nangolo, Makuzayi Massaki or the late Christopher Okigbo, who was killed in action soon after his horn pawed goodbye in 'Elegy for Alto'. Other voices sing of the pains of exile or the anguish of imprisonment. But there is much here that celebrates human love, the abundance of African nature, the surprises of life, the ironies of folly or self-delusion. Laughter resounds as well as tears. No anthology can hope to do more than stimulate the hunger to read and discover more. It must point rather than define, and trust that it has pointed aright.

Angola

Augustinho Neto

Farewell at the Moment of Parting

My mother
(oh black mothers whose children have departed)
you taught me to wait and to hope
as you have done through the disastrous hours

But in me
life has killed that mysterious hope

I wait no more
it is I who am awaited

Hope is ourselves
your children
travelling towards a faith that feeds life

We the naked children of the bush sanzalas
unschooled urchins who play with balls of rags
on the noonday plains
ourselves
hired to burn out our lives in coffee fields
ignorant black men
who must respect the whites
and fear the rich
we are your children of the native quarters
which the electricity never reaches
men dying drunk
abandoned to the rhythm of death's tom-toms
your children
who hunger
who thirst
who are ashamed to call you mother

who are afraid to cross the streets
who are afraid of men

It is ourselves
the hope of life recovered.

African Poem

There on the horizon
the fire
and the dark silhouettes of the imbondeiro trees
with their arms raised
in the air the green smell of burnt palm trees

On the road
the line of Bailundo porters
groaning under their loads of *crueira**

in the room
the sweet sweet-eyed mulatress
retouching her face with rouge and rice-powder
the woman under her many clothes moving her hips
on the bed
the sleepless man thinking
of buying knives and forks to eat with at a table

On the sky the reflections
of the fire
and the silhouette of the blacks at the drums
with their arms raised
in the air the warm tune of marimbas

On the road the porters
in the room the mulatress
on the bed the sleepless man

* *crueira*: maize flour.

The burning coals consuming
consuming with fire
the warm country of the horizons.

Kinaxixi

I was glad to sit down
on a bench in Kinaxixi
at six o'clock of a hot evening
and just sit there . . .

Someone would come
maybe
to sit beside me

And I would see the black faces
of the people going uptown
in no hurry
expressing absence in the
jumbled Kimbundu they conversed in.

I would see the tired footsteps
of the servants whose fathers also were servants
looking for love here, glory there, wanting
something more than drunkenness in every
alcohol.

Neither happiness nor hate.

After the sun had set
lights would be turned on and I
would wander off
thinking that our life after all is simple
too simple
for anyone who is tired and still has to walk.

The Grieved Lands

The grieved lands of Africa
in the tearful woes of ancient and modern slave
in the degrading sweat of impure dance
of other seas
grieved

The grieved lands of Africa
in the infamous sensation of the stunning perfume of the
flower
crushed in the forest
by the wickedness of iron and fire
the grieved lands

The grieved lands of Africa
in the dream soon undone in jinglings of gaolers' keys
and in the stifled laughter and victorious voice of laments
and in the unconscious brilliance of hidden sensations
of the grieved lands of Africa

        Alive
        in themselves and with us alive

They bubble up in dreams
decked with dances by baobabs over balances
by the antelope
in the perpetual alliance of everything that lives

They shout out the sound of life
shout it
even the corpses thrown up by the Atlantic
in putrid offering of incoherence and death
and in the clearness of rivers

They live
the grieved lands of Africa
in the harmonious sound of consciences
contained in the honest blood of men
in the strong desire of men

in the sincerity of men
in the pure and simple rightness of the stars' existence

They live
the grieved lands of Africa
because we are living
and are imperishable particles
of the grieved lands of Africa.

Antonio Jacinto

Monangamba

On that big estate there is no rain
it's the sweat of my brow that waters the crops:

On that big estate there is coffee ripe
and that cherry-redness
is drops of my blood turned sap.

> The coffee will be roasted,
> ground, and crushed,
> will turn black, black with the colour of the *contratado*.*

Black with the colour of the *contratado*!

Ask the birds that sing,
the streams in carefree wandering
and the high wind from inland:

> Who gets up early? Who goes to toil?
> Who is it carries on the long road
> the hammock or bunch of kernels?
> Who reaps and for pay gets scorn
> rotten maize, rotten fish,
> ragged clothes, fifty *angolares*†
> beating for biting back?

Who?

> Who makes the millet grow

---

* *contratado*: contract labourer.
† *angolares*: unit of money.

and the orange groves to flower?
– Who?

Who gives the money for the boss to buy
cars, machinery, women
 and Negro heads for motors?

Who makes the white man prosper,
grow big-bellied – get much money?
– Who?

And the birds that sing,
the streams in carefree wandering
and the high wind from inland
will answer:

 – Monangambeeee . . .

Ah! Let me at least climb the palm trees
Let me drink wine, palm wine
and fuddled by my drunkness forget

 – Monangambeee . . .

Poem of Alienation

 This is not yet my poem
 the poem of my soul and of my blood
 no
 I still lack knowledge and power to write my poem
 the great poem I feel already turning in me

My poem wanders aimlessly
in the bush or in the city
in the voice of the wind
in the surge of the sea
in the Aspect and the Being

My poem steps outside
wrapped in showy cloths
selling itself
selling
   'lemons, buy me le-e-e-emons'

My poem runs through the streets
with a putrid cloth pad on its head
offering itself
offering
   'mackerel, sardine, sprats
   fine fish, fine fi-i-i-sh . . .'

My poem trudges the streets
'here J'urnal' 'Dai-i-i-ly'
and no newspaper yet carries my poem

My poem goes into the cafés
'lott'ry draw-a tomorra lott'ry draw-a tomorra'
and the draw of my poem
wheel as it wheels
whirl as it whirls
never changes
   'lott'ry draw-a tomorra
   lott'ry draw-a tomorra'

My poem comes from the township
on Saturdays bring the washing
on Mondays take the washing
on Saturdays surrender the washing and surrender self
on Mondays surrender self and take the washing

My poem is in the suffering
of the laundress's daughter
shyly
in the closed room
of a worthless boss idling
to build up an appetite for the violation

My poem is the prostitute
in the township at the broken door of her hut

> '*hurry hurry*
> *pay your money*
> *come and sleep with me*'

My poem lightheartedly plays at ball
in a crowd where everyone is a servant
and shouts
> '*offside goal goal*'

My poem is a contract worker
goes to the coffee fields to work
the contract is a burden
that is hard to load
> '*contract wor-r-r-ker*'

My poem walks barefoot in the street

My poem loads sacks in the port
fills holds
empties holds
and finds strength in singing
> '*tué tué tué trr*
> *arrimbuim puim puim*'

My poem goes tied in ropes
met a policeman
paid a fine, the boss
forgot to sign the pass
goes on the roadwork
with hair shorn
> '*head shaved*
> *chicken braised*
> *o Zé*'

a goad that weighs
a whip that plays

My poem goes to market works in the kitchen
goes to the workbench
fills the tavern and the gaol
is poor ragged and dirty

lives in benighted ignorance
my poem knows nothing of itself
nor how to plead

My poem was made to give itself
to surrender itself
without asking for anything

But my poem is not fatalist
my poem is a poem that already wants
and already knows
my poem is I-white
mounted on me-black
riding through life.

Letter from a Contract Worker

I wanted to write you a letter
my love,
a letter that would tell
of this desire
to see you
of this fear
of losing you
of this more than benevolence that I feel
of this indefinable ill that pursues me
of this yearning to which I live in total surrender . . .

I wanted to write you a letter
my love,
a letter of intimate secrets,
a letter of memories of you,
of you
of your lips red as henna
of your hair black as mud
of your eyes sweet as honey
of your breasts hard as wild orange

of your lynx gait
and of your caresses
such that I can find no better here . . .
I wanted to write you a letter
my love,
that would recall the days in our haunts
our nights lost in the long grass
that would recall the shade falling on us from the plum
trees
the moon filtering through the endless palm trees
that would recall the madness
of our passion
and the bitterness
of our separation . . .

I wanted to write you a letter
my love,
that you would not read without sighing
that you would hide from papa Bombo
that you would withhold from mama Kieza
that you would reread without the coldness
of forgetting
a letter to which in all Kilombo
no other would stand comparison . . .

I wanted to write you a letter
my love,
a letter that would be brought to you by the passing wind
a letter that the cashews and coffee trees
the hyenas and buffaloes
the alligators and grayling
could understand
so that if the wind should lose it on the way
the beasts and plants
with pity for our sharp suffering
from song to song
lament to lament
gabble to gabble

would bring you pure and hot
the burning words
the sorrowful words of the letter
I wanted to write to you my love . . .

I wanted to write you a letter . . .

But oh my love, I cannot understand
why it is, why it is, why it is, my dear
that you cannot read
and I – Oh the hopelessness! – cannot write!

Amélia Veiga

Angola

I was not born from your womb
but I loved you each Spring
with the exuberance of a seed . . .

I was not born from your womb
but in you I buried
my longings
and suffered the storm
of a flower transplanted
prematurely . . .

I was not born from your womb
but I drank your charm
in nights of transparent
poetry . . .

I was not born from your womb
but under your shadow
I fertilized new offsprings
and opened my arms
to a transcendent destiny . . .

Angola,
you will not be the land of my birth
but you are the land of my womb.

Costa Andrade

Fourth Poem of a Canto of Accusation

There are on the earth 50,000 dead whom no one mourned
  on the earth
    unburied
      50,000 dead

whom no one mourned.

A thousand Guernicas and the message in the brushes of
Orozco and of Siqueiros
as broad as the sea this silence
spread across the land

    as if the rains had rained blood
    as if the rough hair were grass for many yards
    as if the mouths condemned
    at the very instant of their 50,000 deaths
    all the living of the earth.

There are on the earth 50,000 dead
whom no one mourned

no one . . .

The Mothers of Angola
    have fallen with their sons.

Ngudia Wendel

We Shall Return, Luanda

Luanda, you are like a white seagull
on the ocean crest –
bright streets under the white sun,
flight of green palm trees . . .
but we have seen you grow black, Luanda,
since the bitter fourth of February
when the blood of combatants for liberty
was spilled in your streets –
in your bright streets,
Mother Luanda.

We remember that day
your streets seething with crowds
like the Cuanza in flood.
Our rage thundered louder than the cannon
in the executioner's fortress.

And we went to the attack through a hail of lead
and we died in your streets –
in your bright streets,
Mother Luanda.

Through battle we won victory
on that bitter day,
hundreds of our black brothers
were stretched out for eternity in your streets.

We came through the bush
through the long tropical rains,
the wounded moaned on their stretchers
ammunition belts stained their backs,

legs were caught fast in treacherous swamps,
but we came on to see you,
our Mother Luanda.

But you stranger and hangman
have drowned Luanda in blood,
you have fed on the living body for ages
like the bush tick.
Now you tremble and cling to your sandbags
and steel helmets
and the shelter of machine-guns
wisely, for you know
that the moment of reckoning
is nigh.

One day we shall come out of the bush
through the smoke of the last explosives
and we shall see you, Luanda,
the ships in the bay –
big-bellied ships, hurriedly packed
with the last of the murderers . . .
That day is not over the hills, far away,
it is close at hand
our black brothers give their lives for it.
We shall return, Mother Luanda!

Jofre Rocha

Poem of Return

When I return from the land of exile and silence,
do not bring me flowers.

Bring me rather all the dews,
tears of dawns which witnessed dramas.
Bring me the immense hunger for love
and the plaint of tumid sexes in star-studded night.
Bring me the long night of sleeplessness
with mothers mourning, their arms bereft of sons.

When I return from the land of exile and silence,
no, do not bring me flowers . . .

Bring me only, just this
the last wish of heroes fallen at day-break
with a wingless stone in hand
and a thread of anger snaking from their eyes.

Ruy Duarte de Carvalho

I Come from a South

I came to the east
to gauge the dimension of night
in broad gestures
that I devised in the south
watching flocks and plains
bright
like thighs remembered in May

I come from a south
measured clearly
in transparency of tomorrow's fresh water.
From a circular time
free of seasons.
From a nation of transhumant bodies
blurred
in the colour of the thorned crust
of a black ground chased in live coal.

Makuzayi Massaki

*Regressado,** yes, I am

Regressado, yes I am
For my gestures reveal my ties
to the land of my memory

Regressado, yes I am
For return has always been the goal
of my life in exile

Regressado, yes I am
For it was there from whence I return
that I organized the struggle
to liberate this land

Regressado, yes I am
For my name rhymes with Kimpa Vita,
Nzinga, Buta, Ekwikwi and Mandume†

Regressado, yes I am
For only where my ancestor sleeps
can I build my house

Regressado, yes I am
For I have done nothing else but return
to my point of departure.

---

* Literally, one who returns whence he came; used pejoratively of those returning to
Angola after the War of Independence.
† Heroes of the struggle against Portuguese rule.

Indelible Traces

My crime is to bear the traces
The traces of my culture
The traces of my tradition
So I am the trace
of something that must disappear
but which has survived and left its traces
Good reason for tracking me down
to rub out the trace that I am
in the hope there'll be no more traces of that
But I am not afraid
because that leaves a trace so deep
in the hearts of my people
just as profound as the traces
left in the hearts of men
by that bloody weekend.*

* The weekend of 22 – 24 January 1993, when hundreds of Bakongo were
slaughtered in Luanda by a faction of the MPLA.

Mawete Makisosila

They Told Me

They told me
That I am idle
And anyway
I know nothing of seasons of rest
I know nothing of days of festivity
I lived by forced labour.
They told me
that democracy is a luxury for me
since I have never known it
through all the five centuries of my education
and afterwards,
since I have known nothing but flagellation
and fifteen hours of work per day
during the cursed years.
The curses aimed at me have nourished me
loans and development and democracy
have made me poor
poor in body
poor in mind
and rich in promises from the World Bank
rich in promises from the IMF.
The savings of my abundance
the flourishing youth of my people
are evidence of poverty for the new bosses
and the prophets of nowadays,
but I
I know that I shall live still
so rich in my poverty
and above all, so rich in promises.

Benin

Emile Ologoudou

Vespers

Autumnal skies
the sun has smashed his jar of red oil,
on this day of great anger over the earth
I will leave the dainty lettering of the sky
with
this
message heavy as a bobbin of lead
to tell my people what I am told to tell them,
it is the fixed invective of the other shore
and
the heart at this work for the rest of my life,
I shall see no more this sun which totters,
this light which crumples under the slow shadows,
ah!
what are they these things which capsize
in
the sea of my being at the hour of departure?
it is, at the very summit of the soul,
terror before the thousand promises we shall be able to keep.

Liberty

The white carcases
of
ships .
sought desperately
the visible island with its golden mist,

the native isle of insurrection,
stage at evening of the most tragic adventures,
we were tossed
on the waves of the same sorrow,
and discord
had not yet blown towards us the sands
of
its evidence,
exuberance still reigned over the happy bay,
that day when we made long funerals
for all the things
we had to bury . . .

Botswana

Barolong Seboni

Love that

inner sense
of innocence
that craves eternally
the momentary
experience in
the oneness
of
twosome.

memory

life is but memories unborn

the world revolves
like a cranium
on the neck of time
we remember; we forget
then we die
hoping to become eternal
memories yet unborn.

between the begetting
and the forgetting,
in memory lies life.

Cameroon

Simon Mpondo

The Season of the Rains

The season of the rains
Signs its name in a thousand fashions
Those who want to read omens there
Will find their signs
In the flowering beard of the maize
And in the black or red rings of millipedes
Does the swallow's departure for the Margui-Wandala
Announce many storms and floods along the Wouri?
Has the spider woven its web
Stored up insects and light and the sun's warmth
To vanquish a cold season of a thousand days?
Does the plucked chicken speak of hard or easy times?

What says the black millipede?
What says the red millipede?
They say what the omens say
Yes or no or even perhaps
These are the signs
But they tell mainly what happened in the dry season
And not what the rains will bring forth
Plenty of labour in the dry days
Translates itself as maize in the wet
And in food for millipede's colour
And the largeness of its rings
Which the sorcerer measures in his secret hut
Owe nothing to the season
Those colours will always vary
Some rings will always be large
And some narrow

Let each person make of it what he will
The signs of the rainy season
Say exactly what everyone wants to hear
Surely there will be plenty of water
Plenty of swamps and mud
That's the message we read in the signs
Of the season of rains.

Mbella Sonne Dipoko

Our Life

An ailing bird over the desert made its agony
A song blown through the air
As at the oasis
Drawers of water said
How low it flies oh how touching its song

The winged hope that proved to be a dream
(Masked our destiny with a black hood)

As in the cities we said the same prayers
As in the villages we espoused ancestral myths
Transmitting our frustration our life our mortality
To the young country of tomorrow and day after tomorrow
Flattering ourselves with the charity of the blood-donor's love.

Pain

All was quiet in this park
Until the wind, like a gasping messenger, announced
The tyrant's coming
Then did the branches talk in agony.
You remember that raging storm?

In their fear despairing flowers nevertheless held
Bouquets to the grim king;
Meteors were the tassels of his crown
While like branches that only spoke when the storm menaced
We cried in agony as we fell
Slashed by the cold blade of an invisible sword.

Mutilated, our limbs were swept away by the rain;
But not our blood;
Indelible, it stuck on the walls
Like wild gum on tree-trunks.

Exile

In silence
The overloaded canoe leaves our shores

But who are these soldiers in camouflage,
These clouds going to rain in foreign lands?

The night is losing its treasures
The future seems a myth
Warped on a loom worked by lazy hands.

But perhaps all is not without some good for us
As from the door of a shack a thousand miles away
The scaly hand of a child takes in greeting
The long and skinny fingers of the rain.

A Poem of Villeneuve St Georges
(for M–C)

I am tempted to think of you
Now that I have grown old
And date my sadness
To the madness of your love.

All those flowers you hung
On my gate
All those flowers the wind blew
On the snow!
Why must I remember them now
And recall you calling me
Like a screech-owl

While I watched you
Through the window-pane
And the moon was over the Seine
And Africa was far away
And you were calling
And then crying
In the snow of exile
And the neighbour's dog barking as if bored
By the excesses of your tenderness?

When I came down for you
And opened the gate
Cursing the cold of your land
You always went and stood
Under the poplars of the river Yerres
At the bottom of the garden
Silently watching its Seine-bound waters;
And the moon might take to the clouds
Casting a vast shadow
That sometimes seemed to reach our hearts.

And then following me upstairs
You stopped a while on the balcony
As high as which the vines of the garden grew
With those grapes which had survived
The end of the summer
You picked a few grapes
Which we ate.
I remember their taste
Which was that of our kisses.

And then in the room
You in such a hurry to undress
And you always brought
A white and a black candle which you lit.
Their flames were the same colour
Of the fire glowing in the grate
And you were no longer white
You were brown

By the light of the fires of love
At midnight
Years ago.

From My Parisian Diary

Thirty centimes is all the money I have left
But I am full of hope without knowing why
I laugh at the world and laugh at myself
Something of a child at thirty-five.
It has been a hard life since I ran out of cynicism
And stopped selling for a commission
Just any newspaper in the world
Deciding exclusively on pamphlets of the Left
By which I am now earning death by instalment
On a starvation diet
And the rent is long overdue.
Surely this is not a way of earning a living
Peddling slogans of a better world
In the garrison of troops armed to defend these cruel days.
But the struggle must continue
And we must open new fronts even in our dreams.

Patrice Kayo

Song of the Initiate

All the wives of my father
      pulled my mother to bits
But their children cannot dance
It is I who have taken my father's stool
And my mother has become queen
All the wives of my father my wives
      and servants of my mother.

The mother of those who cannot dance
      has never borne children
Her children are nothing but epileptics
      The initiate alone with the chief.

If only I were a river!
I would roll down all silvery
And in the compound of the non-initiate
      I would become a swamp.

I am only a dealer in pigs
      and in chickens
But if you have any pearls or little bells
      I will buy them.
The only son alone
Is sure of his father's stool.
The panther's child does not fear the night
I can dance all the dances
And my mother eats nothing but the flesh of sparrowhawks.

War

Thunderous vapours!
water-spout with lion's teeth

A trumpet sounds the end of things
with its scabby tongue

But no, but no
The forests and mountains are still calving
and in his velvety pot
God sleeps on his anvil

Tossing fate to the winds
gun at the ready
the Orphan man goes forth
with his thoughts on his nose

At the market where one grinds one's teeth
stamp
lacerate yourself
We have ground our teeth
stamped
and lacerated ourselves
And it was our destiny.

For the altar of expiation
we would be the incense
and awaken God from his coma
Let him abolish us
And begin his creation afresh
Let him shatter science
extinguish the embers
And plunge us again in the sweetness
of innocent day.

For man if you pass
from God's vassal to his equal
and if upon the scaffold
You decapitate death
the new God
You would still be no less monstrous.

Cape Verde Islands

Onésimo Silveira

A Different Poem

The people of the islands want a different poem
For the people of the islands;
A poem without exiles complaining
In the calm of their existence;
A poem without children nourished
On the black milk of aborted time
A poem without mothers gazing
At the vision of their sons, motherless.
The people of the islands want a different poem
For the people of the islands:
A poem without arms in need of work
Nor mouths in need of bread
A poem without boasts ballasted with people
On the road to the South
A poem without words choked
By the harrows of silence.
The people of the islands want a different poem
For the people of the islands:
A poem with sap rising in the heart of the BEGINNING
A poem with Batuque and tchabeta and the badias of St Catherine,
A poem with shaking hips and laughing ivory.
The people of the islands want a different poem
For the people of the islands:
A poem without men who lose the seas' grace
and the fantasy of the main compass points.

Congo Republic (Congo-Brazzaville)

Tchicaya U Tam'si

Three poems from *Feu de brousse* (1957)

Brush Fire

The fire the river that's to say
the sea to drink following the sand
the feet the hands
within the heart to love
this river that lives in me repeoples me
only to you I said around the fire

my race
it flows here and there a river
the flames are the looks
of those who brood upon it
I said to you
my race
remembers
the taste of bronze drunk hot.

Dance to the Amulets

Come over here
our grass is rich
come you fawns

gestures and stabs of sickly hands
curving then unripping of conception
one – who? – you shape my fate
come you fawns

over here the suppleness of mornings
and the blood masked here
and the rainbow-coloured dream the rope at the neck
come over here

our grass is rich here
my first coming
was the harsh explosion of a flint
solitude
my mother promised me to light.

A Mat to Weave

he came to deliver the secret of the sun
and wanted to write the poem of his life

why crystals in his blood
why globules in his laughter

his soul was ready
when someone called him
dirty wog

still he is left with the gentle arch of his laughter
and the giant tree with a living cleft
what was that country where he lived a beast
behind the beasts before behind the beasts

his stream was the safest of cups
because it was of bronze
because it was his living flesh

it was then that he said to himself
no my life is not a poem .

here is the tree here is the water here are the stones
and then the priest of the future

it is better to love wine
and rise in the morning
he was advised

but no more birds within the tenderness of mothers
dirty wog
he is the younger brother to fire

the bush begins here
and the sea is no more than the memory of gulls
all standing upright tooth-to-tooth
against the spume of a deadly dance
the tree was the leafiest
the bark of the tree was the tenderest
after the forest was burnt what more to say

why was there absinthe in the wine
why restore in the hearts
the crocodiles the canoers
and the wave of the stream
the grains of sand between the teeth
is it thus that one breaks the world
no
no
his stream was the gentlest of cups
the safest
it was his most living flesh

here begins the poem of his life
he was trained in a school
he was trained in a studio
and he saw roads planted with sphinxes

still he is left with the soft arch of his laughter
then the tree then the water then the leaves

that is why you will see him
the marching canoers have raised once more
against the haulers of french cotton
their cries
this flight is a flight of doves

the leeches did not know the bitterness
of this blood
in the purest of cups

dirty gollywog
behold my congolese head

it is the purest of cups.

Four poems from *Épitomé* (1962)

A bouquet of faded flowers in my letterbox . . .

> I was naked for the first kiss of my mother
> I was naked before Sammy and before men
>
> I would be cold already
> Without this taste of black salt
> in your black blood
>
> I have the claws of a woman in my flesh
> I bleed for her delight in love
> But hide from me the image of her god
> that fakir whose grin desalts my soul
> and lets the ferns
> hold in the earth
> the freshness of a patch of violent water.

These flowers in my letterbox, I cross my fingers to caress them and the
conscience of the world is silent with me over the drama of Léopoldville –
I spit into the Seine like all good poets.

> What do I want with a thousand stars in broad daylight
> the rapt surrealist
> in one of them at midnight
> has blessed my crazy reason
>
> My reason is the memory of a levitation
> it knits a blue stocking for the violated night
> it kindles hell in the black flames it ends
> the purification of my sinful swan
> which once fixed a halo of pollen
>
> on the head of a lustful black crab
> my reason makes me difficult and faithless
> in the abstract of my passion.

My prick is not even a root of the tree,
to speak as that tree rustles
would give a rustic perfume
to the game of my flight
and put less blood on the hands of my quest.

The disasters unfold in silence
as one loved them in childhood memory
and a grey rain serves all our dreams
forcing me to become a forger
and holy assassin
despite the equinox
despite myself
despite the sorcery of the smiles
of my obedient black brothers

And then
what would you have me say of this silence
squatting beside my own conscience?

They give you what they have eaten and what they have not known how
to keep. The shadow, like them, had a certain reticence.
I am full of spite with the sun.

You must be from my country
I see it by the tick
of your soul around the eyelashes
and besides you dance when you are sad
you must be from my country

Keep moving time is waiting to seduce us
learn from this that the oil in your lamp
is really my blood brimming up
and that, if it overflows, you mustn't light your lamp
we must have a dark corner somewhere
for our ancient orisons

All of us from the same umbilical cord
But who knows where we fetch
our awkward heads

Often the silences
reeking of iodine ravage us
with lecherous resolves
for my beardless conscience
ravage us alone.

The Scorner

I drink to your glory my god
You who have made me so sad
You have given me a people who are not distillers of gin

What wine shall I drink to your *jubilate*
In this country which has no vines
In this desert all the bushes are of cactus
Shall I take their crop of flowers
for flames of the burning bush of your desire
Tell me in what Egypt my people's feet lie chained

Christ I laugh at your sadness
O my sweet Christ
Thorn for thorn
We have a common crown of thorns
I will be converted because you tempt me
Joseph comes to me
I suck already the breast of the Virgin your mother
I count more than your one Judas on my fingers
My eyes lie to my soul
Where the world is a lamb your pascal lamb – Christ
I will waltz to the tune of your slow sadness.

Two poems from *Le Ventre* (1964)

1

                    'The Congo is myself' (Lumumba)

I myself will be the stage for my salvation!
Already velvet breaks the silences
with evanescent wings
which snow upon the oil-lamp.

Slobber within the masks will serve better for this carnival
than grinning on a thousand different notes,
But since I have only one face
Over that alone shall I pass my hand.
The flat horizon of this country splits my heart
If I recoil everything bristles suddenly!
I will stay at the gate with the wind in my side
but with tornadoes in my belly

2

I tear at my belly,
Neither seawrack nor iodine
nor the very algae have so much
tenderness in their caress
as my lips knew once
before the earth was insulted
by a galloping herd of ventriloquist jackals!

The belly
always with that sickening warmth
as of the charnel-house.

From L'Arc musical (1970)

Epitaph

We are this union
of water salt and earth
of sunshine and flesh
bespattering the sun
no more among the sea marks
but because there is this song
which ruins all the gulfs
which recreates a genesis
of wind weather and flesh!

I predict a babel
of unoxidized steel
or of crossed blood
mixed in the dregs of all surges!
After the red man,
after the black man,
after the yellow man,
after the white man,
there is already the man of bronze
sole alloy of the soft fires
we have still to ford.

Legacy

The singing violin
has not burnt the wind
when a procession of raw bones
snows wildly upon us

A hesitant love
pours nothing over our labours
but an icy shower of gold
gnawing away
the last warm sigh
anonymously

And as always
the earth more ardently
wishing us at rest
within her milkless sides
will lap us with humus.

And if this harp cannot follow me
there where the spirits wait
This is my testament:
I leave you the fire and the song.

Jean-Baptiste Tati-Loutard

Four poems from *Poèmes de la mer* (1968)

News of My Mother

I am now very high upon the tree of the seasons;
Far below I see the firm earth of the past.
When the fields opened themselves to the flow of seed
Before the baobab took aim at a flight of birds
With the first call of the sun,
It was your footsteps which sang around me:
A shower of bells chiming with my ablutions.
I am now very high upon the tree of the seasons.
Know by this fifteenth day of the moon
It is these tears – up till now –
Which fill your absence,
Which lighten drop by drop your image
Too heavy on my pupil;
Each night I waken drenched through with your pain
Even as if you lived in me again.

The Voices

Far across the waves, the wing of a gull
Ventilates a sea full of impurities –
The insult and darkness of refusal –
I remember it through the navel
Which ties me to the centuries of wrong.
The sea has assembled all their bones
Under the cross of the reefs;

They sleep their black oceanic slumber
In the heavy shroud of the silent deeps.
But I have an eye to pierce the darkness
Better than the fine fingers of sunlight
And an ear which hears the groans
Even the squalls cannot disperse,
An ear which catches the sound of a plunge
The stillest waters cannot cover.

Submarine Tombs

With my sevenfold inquisitorial eye,
More obscene than the urban wind,
I have raised up through its ripping folds
A dress of blue snake-skin
Horrible! All the side of a race
Lies there, spent,
Across the huge blocks of the generations.

Our liberty still weighs upon us
Seaweed and coral brothers
Who have never ceased to watch over our dead.
One day we will reward your constancy as it deserves,
And for their funerals we will dry up the sea.

Pilgrimage to Loango Strand

I have followed to this strand the scent of their blood
Of my blood
Forgetting other scars burnt by the hard wind
In days gone by; here I'll stop:
Life sickens me; I will go no further.
Even the path falters before the memory-post
Of an embarcation.
The sea still describes infinity

To this harbour, rocking its pendulum
Through three centuries;
And God's spirit still circles above the waters
Of this great flat silence
Pecked by the voyaging gulls.
I shall not continue my pilgrimage
Over the submarine roadway paved with bones
Until the distant resurgence of Jamestown
Amid the camps of death flowered with cotton.
Let noble Africa raise its own cenotaphs
For the repose of those heavy-hearted dead
Who went spilling their bitterness
Over the spume of the waves.

Two poems from Les Racines congolaises (1968)

Noonday in Immaturity

With a dozen blows the clock betrays the pulse of time,
And the day-forged sun
Now begins its retreat amid a blaze of sparks.
The walls of races, of banks, of asylums
Blind me; I watch; far away
A single gap opens in the wall of fate,
Far off far off, it's the vast estuary of death
Where all my daily dreams converge.
As all the poems of my immaturity flare up
I will keep the ashes of their death on my face
Until the new germination.
I feel myself lonely and slender in the mirror of the lightning.

The tree my friend turns down his wick
Which watched over my thirst for the shadows;
I go forth in the sunlight
And, diviner with empty bag, I walk painfully
Through the fires of the centre.

Death and Rebirth

May the hide of the earth split beneath my feet,
May the valve of the sky open and show me
The high niche of the sun or the immense reach of the stars.
I shall fear nothing.

Does Death call me? Will it at least offer me
A mirror, a sheet of light where I can glimpse
My profile beyond the grave?

I am a seeding branch of this world,
My dreams flourish in the sunlight
Not in the gloomy swarming of the molluscs,
I balance myself in the wind;

I dizzy myself with all the gifts of day and night,
In passing I pluck the drunken birds from space: take them!
The serpent comes here each morning to my patch of dew

To lap at the source of his cry!
Like him, I throw myself ever higher and further,
No one sees how I prosper in the shadow of my secret;
I shall not respond to that call which rises from the thickets
Of the night.

Let the sea flow back upon itself with its cargo
Of salt and fishes! Let the sky split its azure lining!
Let the sun burst in a tourniquet of fire!
Why shouldn't it start with the elements?
I am at the dawn of a people beginning a long march:
I shall see them break from their coop in all the sweat
Of their souls, as the sun breaks from the channels of the East
In a great transpiration of Light!

From *La Tradition du songe* (1985)

Secret Destiny

The sun unveils beneath the sky's circle
A land of rivers and forests
A woman of savage virtue
Dishevelled by brackish breezes
Who purges us of world-weariness
I open myself to its great waters
Which turn aside to flow through my dream
I become their bed of clay
They can flood at leisure
And scatter with gems
Like those collars of stars
Thrown round the neck of night
It's a land of firm earth
Bristled with a frizzy volcanic race
yelling for their freedom
Like a sun which gives birth to a tide-rip
Congo moulded with a slime that spreads
beneath the feet of pachyderm tyrants
Sometimes you pose as an extinct volcano
And you converse with your destiny
Still mingled with the night which strides
With invisible steps crushing
All the stones of the Milky Way

Two poems from *Le Serpent austral* (1992)

End of Flight

I

At last man has seen the death of the free bird
Over the sands mingled with sea-wrack
The nude-necked predator showed himself
Beating his wings thrice
And losing height he resumed
His long strokes across the waves
The sea lifted him with its misty breath
Like the fruit of its own entrails
And through a hole opened in the wind
The bird has shot once more
See him returning to the shore
Calmly disdaining the spoil thrown up
By the tide since nightfall
The call of the deep must have sounded within him
For the flight of his damnation
Buffeted by the coastal breeze
His slanted gaze surveying
A boat like an islet
And man has followed bird until his final plunge

II

Behold the predator of naked neck
Now but a plaything of the waves
He swims and doesn't know it
He dances and doesn't feel it
Time was shattered in his fall
Spreading its days across the spume
Like the bird's feathers
Drawn back to the maternal breast
Before the hawk's harsh destiny

The man has never quitted the strand
He follows from there the ball tossed by the waves
And night falls like a shell
Blasting the sea

Letter to Edouard Maunick

I knew it from the moment I heard of your coming
The Congo couldn't leave you intact
He who bears the bites of a crazy lover
Like you I bear the sickness of river and ocean
When I hear the waves from afar
My heart lifts with the billows
Ready to offer the ocean my nautilic soul
I certainly don't feel that I'm made of slime
Even if I resemble a clay pot
I need exile your great exile
If I am to weep every night for the waves
O mystery of the beetle who was a god
I roll no ball of waste or of dung
The drizzle gives me fevers
I bird of the high winds born like you
From the violent breath of blue waters.

Emmanuel Dongala

Fantasy under the Moon
(Blues for a muted trumpet)

I climbed towards you on a ray of moonlight
that filtered through a hole in my straw-thatched house
When I had reached the smiling arch of your mouth among the
    stars
you came to me
open under the sea of your body the heaving wave under my body
my heart beating to the rhythm of yours moving to the rhythm of
    your tribe the people of the mountain;
your serpent form writhing beneath mine
I sucked your cobra's poison from your broken lips
and my fever mounted like a sickness.

I visited last night our banana grove of the first time.
When I reached those great sombre aisles
under which we pressed each other behind your mother's back
under the teasing trumpet of thirsty mosquitoes
the circle of my arms about your shadow your phantom
all at once hung emptier than the rope of a wine-tapper
embracing the palm tree.

I don't know why that large cloud crossing the moon
suddenly made the tide of your body fall.
Like oiled wrestlers at a festival
who feel their adversary slide between their arms
powerless I felt you slip from mine
under the moon's light white as this wine as your teeth which made
    you so gay

as you fluttered wildly in the circle of the dance
while your mother warned you not to come near me.

I looked up at the sky from the depths of my hut;
the moon was only a smile, your white smile congealed.

Côte d'Ivoire

Joseph Miezan Bognini

From *Ce dur appel de l'espoir* (1960)

My Days Overgrown

My days overgrown with coffee blossoms,
My childhood has lost its meaning.

The hatred one has eaten
Can never be destroyed.

Misfortune, I am misfortune,
And my shadow has betrayed me;
Suffering, I am suffering,
Inexperienced at the breast of mankind.

I wish you were music
Rocking the thirsty hearts from afar.

You will carry me away one day
Wrapped in white robes
Into another world.

I have become a grain of sand
Drifting along trembling beaches.

You will bring me asylum
That knows the pain of this night.

You changed your face,
I took you by the hand

And we spent happy days.

Earth and Sky

Earth and sky are infinities
Where our cries cannot venture

I have fixed my head between two stones
Seeking the Shelterer in vain.

Only your splendour sets me free

I have run through the void
Crossing a thousand villages

Where could I draw breath
Without damaging your scenery?

The nights have flayed me
Like a careless wanderer.

I am simply an insect
Without wings or paws

Scornful serpents are my only fare

Heat crackles upon my roof
The ripe fruit of my flesh is shrinking

Love lies crumpled at my feet.
I would strip myself of all my cares
And wear the dress of consolation only.

Such joy is new to me.

I will take you for my companion
My body is lost in your arms.

But make me insensate as the wind
Which strikes and ravages nature,
Not to make me hate you
But to love you always.

Two poems from *Herbe féconde* (1973)

1

We are men of the new world a tree prompts us to harmony
  A tree whose fruit is pulpy
  It isn't the tree of good or evil but that of concupiscence.
  Whose fruit was flung on our shoulders at the dawn of our
solicitude and ranged at evening in the freezing spaces of an
infallible cuisine!
  The silence plays with us. And our aptitudes in this time seized
with firmness rejoice at an audience stooped before the reason
justice triumphantly brandishes.
  We are men of the intensest heat
  Matter fashioned from resonance
  Multiplied souls
  Lanterns of immortal light
  Lands of unutterable representation

2

  Suddenly an old man on the threshold of the age. A wind comes
to swell the despoiled year.
  White sands with brownish stocks, Roots excited by the heat.
Delirious paths where the night's hypnosis flies;
  I prop myself for a moment on the slope of his pure face and
turn my body
  My lamb's vehemence in the suave musicality of his decayed
loins and it is fidelity which pricks the awakening skin
  Abundance of fluid which spurs the nuptial dance:
  The peasant dreams of his cabbage feet
  The epicurean walker swifter than the wind
  The crowd explodes with joy and eulogies
  Passage of tender gleams under the storm, the skylight opens
upon a lucrative seeding
  The granaries will protect their fortunes
  I glimpse a luminous ending

Like an alleged transmission
    And the bonds of survival offered forever
Sustenance will attain the summit of intensity
    Suddenly the old man on the threshold of the age hoists with his
superb hand the leaf of spontaneity.

Charles Nokan

My Head is Immense

My head is immense
I have a toad's eyes
A horn stands on the nape of my neck
But a magical music surges
from me.
What tree exhales such rare
perfume?
Dark beauty, how can you spring
from a toad's wallow? How can you
flow from lonely ugliness?
You who look on, you think
that the voice of my instrument
buys my freedom, that I am fluidity, thought
which flies.
No, there is nothing in me
but a pool of sadness.

Democratic Republic of Congo (Congo-Kinshasa)

Antoine-Roger Bolamba

Portrait

I have my gri-gri
        gri-gri
        gri-gri
my calm bounding awake
clings to the wavy limbs of the Congo
never a stormy passage for my heart
bombarded with glowing oriflammes
I think of my silver necklace
become a hundred isles of silence
I admire the obstinate patience
of the okapi
bluebird battered in the open sky
what shipwreck
plunges it to the gulf of nothingness
nothingness empty of nightly entreaties

Ah! the broken resolutions
ah! the screaming follies
let my fate fall upon its guardians
they are three villains

I say three in counting 1 2 3
who dim the ancestral mirror
but you fugitive image
I will see you on the height of dizzy anger
wait while I put on my brow my mask of blood
and soon you will see
my tongue flutter like a banner.

A Fistful of News

The hills hunch their backs
and leap above the marshes
that wash about the calabash
of the Great Soul

Rumours of treason spread
like burning swords
the veins of the earth
swell with nourishing blood
the earth bears
towns villages hamlets
forests and woods
peopled with monsters horned and tentacled
their long manes are the mirror of the Sun

they are those who when night has come
direct the regiments of bats
and who sharpen their arms
upon the stone of horror.

the souls of the guilty
float in the currents of air
on the galleys of disaster
paying no heed to the quarrels of the earthbound
with fangs of fire
they tear from the lightning its diamond heart.

Surely the scorn is a gobbet of smoking flesh
surely the spirits recite the rosary of vengeance
but like the black ear of wickedness
they have never understood a single word
of the scorpion's obscure tongue:
stubbornness

nor the anger of the snake-wizard
nor the violence of the throwing-knife
can do anything against it.

Mukula Kadima-Nzuji

Incantations of the Sea: Moando Coast

Shocks of dizziness
my waves, my fears of the ocean
on the salty strand of my desire.

Shocks of carnal dreams
my heaps of loosened cliff
in the bitter absence
of sap mounting to the brim of the foam.

Loosened my pollens of drunkenness
and tied and retied my seaweeds
milky way of destinies.

And I hear
stooped over the virgin insomnia
of altitudes
the savage cries of the sea
and the rough backwash of my being.

Love in the Plural

neither this sobbing ocean
in the moon of your swelling voice
nor the milky vapour
on the window of my waking
nor this flood of men
in the margin of my shadow
which yearns for a safe shelter

nor the slipstreams on camelback
in the desert of my solitude
nor the spindrift nor the seaweeds
pillows for my storm-filled head
are able to decipher
where I inspect myself in vain
the reverse side of mirrors.

Gambia

Lenrie Peters

Homecoming

The present reigned supreme
　　Like the shallow floods over the gutters
Over the raw paths where we had been,
　　The house with the shutters.

Too strange the sudden change
　　Of the times we buried when we left
The times before we had properly arranged
　　The memories that we kept.

Our sapless roots have fed
　　The wind-swept seedlings of another age.
Luxuriant weeds have grown where we led
　　The Virgins to the water's edge.

There at the edge of the town
　　Just by the burial ground
Stands the house without a shadow
　　Lived in by new skeletons.

That is all that is left
　　To greet us on the home-coming
After we have paced the world
　　And longed for returning.

Song

Clawed green-eyed
Feline of night
Palsy-breasted
Selling old boot
On wet pavement
In hour-glass baskets
Coconut bellied
Unyielding copra
Gland exhausted
Love fatigued
Worm-tunnelled sod
Prostituted fruit of Eve
Edging the Park trees
Like dancing Caterpillars
In folded leaves
Softened by Social Conscience
Hounded by Prudes
Friend of the falling star
Victim of the lonely bed.

We Have Come Home

We have come home
From the bloodless war
With sunken hearts
Our boots full of pride –
From the true massacre of the soul
When we have asked
'What does it cost
To be loved and left alone?'

We have come home,
Bringing the pledge
Which is written in rainbow colours

Across the sky – for burial
But it is not the time
To lay wreaths
For yesterday's crimes
Night threatens
Time dissolves
And there is no acquaintance
With tomorrow
The gurling drums
Echo the star
The forest howls –
And between the trees
The dark sun appears.

We have come home
When the dawn falters
Singing songs of other lands
The Death March
Violating our ears
Knowing all our lore and tears
Determined by the spinning coin.

We have come home
To the green foothills
To drink from the cry
Of warm and mellow birdsong.
To the hot beaches
Where boats go out to sea
Threshing the ocean's harvest
And the harassing, plunging
Gliding gulls shower kisses on the waves.
We have come home

Where through the lightning flash
And thundering rain
The Pestilence, the drought
The sodden spirit
Lingers on the sandy road

Supporting the tortured remnants
Of the flesh
That spirit which asks no favour
But to have dignity.

One Long Jump

One long jump
From the early days
When the face was like a globe
Round, revolving, limitless
Sharp incisive like a probe
And eyes which could see
With the completeness of a globe – geometrically
A soft film of brown hairs
And a language of birds and flowers.

One long jump
From the early days
When wave upon wave
Of passion merged
Cutting their losses
Preserving their 'gains'
And beauty tingled the flesh
Like a snake
On the surface of the lake
Yielding her store of comfort
Without deceit
Without fictitious powers of support
And no didactic analyses
To know that milk was sweet.

One long jump
And never another
Never quite the same
Because things get mouldy
In the grave

And milk loses its taste
On the coated tongue
Bartered birthrite
Like the chaste membrane
Is lost for good
So we can never arrive
At the beginning
To couch in the blue light
Of the primaeval hive
Except in the dissolution of the flesh
And early strength never returns
To oppose the grinding artificialities
Or to marvel at the rose

One long jump
The first and last
And no progression
So take it well.
Looking back upsets
The balanced wheel
Too tired if we arrive
It is enough
To seek the short cut
To the grave.

Parachute Men

Parachute Men say
The first jump
Takes the breath away
Feet in the air disturbs
Till you get used to it.

Solid ground
Is not where you left it
As you plunge down
Perhaps head first

As you listen to
Your arteries talking
You learn to sustain hope

Suddenly you are only
Holding an open umbrella
In a windy place
As the warm earth
Reaches out to you
Reassures you
The vibrating interim is over

You try to land
Where the green grass yields
And carry your pack
Across the fields.

The violent arrival
Puts out the joint
Earth has nowhere to go
You are at the starting point

Jumping across worlds
In condensed time
After the awkward fall
We are always at the starting point.

Isatou Died

Isatou died
When she was only five
And full of pride
Just before she knew
How small a loss
It brought to such a few.
Her mother wept
Half grateful
To be so early bereft.

And did not see the smile
As tender as the root
Of the emerging plant
Which sealed her eyes.
The neighbours wailed
As they were paid to do
And thought how big a spread
Might be her wedding too.
The father looked at her
Through marble eyes and said;
'Who spilt the perfume
Mixed with morning dew?'

Tijan Sallah

The Coming Turning

The coming is the turning,
Weep not like birds
With scattered nestlings.

We know it
By the silence of our children
And the unsettled of our fishy selves.

The coming is in the morning,
Not like herds of cattle
Heading through appetite-gates,
Or like gazelles, running wildly
Into tangled bushpath, forgetting
The route they came through.

The coming approaches
Through the patient anticipation
Of children. It comes, comes,
Quietly to meet our anxious desires.

We will know the when of the turning.
The moonlight will reveal
The erratic flashes of our past,
The kingly betrayals, the
Tumultuous sufferings.

We know the coming is the turning,
When the fences crumble
On the grasshoppers and locusts,
When we handshake with
The warmth of our hearts.

Sahelian Earth

This season is for the baobabs.
Baobabs are princes of height.
Their swollen feet command
A whole empire under earth.

Above the baobabs,
Seagulls dive in and out of brackish waters.
They stare at us with country-bred eyes.
They stare at us like Serere fishermen from Joal.

The sun radiates above splinter boughs.
This is a season of desolate laughters.
Very little warm water has fallen
To comfort our souls.
Very little water has fallen
On palmfronds to support
The throat of crows.

Rains have signed a contract of neglect
With our landscape. Rains have signed a contract of neglect.
Our soils are bare, without grass or shrubs,
Without weeds or creepers. Our inheritance
Has suddenly turned into
The restless despair of the camel's fate.

Only the baobabs stride majestically
In our landscape; their octopus branches
Cling to some ancient hope.

We sweat till our bodies shrivel like bonga fish.
We sweat to cool off our body fires.
Sweat is catharsis for us.
God pours down cold water from the inside.

Ghana

Ellis Ayitey Komey

The Change

Your infancy now a wall of memory
In harmattan the locusts filled the sky
Destroying the sweat put into the field
And restless seas shattered canoes
The fisher-folk put to sail by noon.
The impatience in your teens
Yet silent were your dreams
With the fires in your heart
Breaking the mask of innocence.
The evasive solitude in your womb
And the determination of your limbs
With eyes like the soaring eagle
Shattering the glass of ignorance.
Your infancy now a wall of memory
Before this you, like the worms,
Leaning on for vain indecorous dreams
And the cobras with venomous tongues
Licking the tepid blooms of hibiscus.

Oblivion

I want to remember the fallen palm
With whitening fluid of wine
Dripping from its hardened belly
In this forest of life.

I want to remember it from the road
With mud on my feet,
And thorn-scraped flesh
From the branches by the water.

I want to remember them well
The sight of the green-eyed forest
The jubilant voices of the frogs
And the pleading cries of the owls.

I want to walk among the palms
With their razor-edged leaves
Shadowing the yam and cassava shrubs
Under which the crab builds its castle
And the cocoa pods drooping like mothers
Breasts feeding a hungry child.

I want to remember them all
Before they die and turn to mud
When I have gone.

Kwesi Brew

A Plea for Mercy

We have come to your shrine to worship –
We the sons of the land.
The naked cowherd has brought
The cows safely home,
And stands silent with his bamboo flute
Wiping the rain from his brow;
As the birds brood in their nests
Awaiting the dawn with unsung melodies;
The shadows crowd on the shores
Pressing their lips against the bosom of the sea;
The peasants home from their labours
Sit by their log fires
Telling tales of long ago.
Why should we the sons of the land
Plead unheeded before your shrine,
When our hearts are full of song
And our lips tremble with sadness?
The little firefly vies with the star,
The log fire with the sun
The water in the calabash
With the mighty Volta.
But we have come in tattered penury
Begging at the door of a Master.

The Search

The past
Is but the cinders
Of the present;
The future
The smoke
That escaped
Into the cloud-bound sky.

Be gentle, be kind, my beloved
For words become memories,
And memories tools
In the hands of jesters.
When wise men become silent,
It is because they have read
The palms of Christ
In the face of the Buddha.

So look not for wisdom
And guidance
In their speech, my beloved.
Let the same fire
Which chastened their tongues
Into silence,
Teach us – teach us!

The rain came down,
When you and I slept away
The night's burden of our passions;
Their new-found wisdom
In quick lightning flashes
Revealed the truth
That they had been
The slaves of fools.

Kofi Awoonor

Songs of Sorrow

Dzogbese Lisa has treated me thus
It has led me among the sharps of the forest
Returning is not possible
And going forward is a great difficulty
The affairs of this world are like the chameleon faeces
Into which I have stepped
When I clean it cannot go.*

I am on the world's extreme corner,
I am not sitting in the row with the eminent
But those who are lucky
Sit in the middle and forget
I am on the world's extreme corner
I can only go beyond and forget.

My people, I have been somewhere
If I turn here, the rain beats me
If I turn there, the sun burns me
The firewood of this world
Is only for those who can take heart
That is why not all can gather it.
The world is not good for anybody
But you are so happy with your fate;
Alas! the travellers are back
All covered with debt.

Something has happened to me
The things so great that I cannot weep;

* Colloquial: It [the faeces] will not go [come off].

I have no sons to fire the gun when I die
And no daughters to wail when I close my mouth
I have wandered on the wilderness
The great wilderness men call life
The rain has beaten me,
And the sharp stumps cut as keen as knives
I shall go beyond and rest.
I have no kin and no brother,
Death has made war upon our house;

And Kpeti's great household is no more,
Only the broken fence stands;
And those who dared not look in his face
Have come out as men.
How well their pride is with them.
Let those gone before take note
They have treated their offspring badly.
What is the wailing for?
Somebody is dead. Agosu himself
Alas! a snake has bitten me
My right arm is broken,
And the tree on which I lean is fallen.

Agosu if you go tell them,
Tell Nyidevu, Kpeti, and Kove
That they have done us evil;
Tell them their house is falling
And the trees in the fence
Have been eaten by termites;
That the martels curse them.
Ask them why they idle there
While we suffer, and eat sand,
And the crow and the vulture
Hover always above our broken fences
And strangers walk over our portion.

Song of War

I shall sleep in white calico;
War has come upon the sons of men
And I shall sleep in calico;
Let the boys go forward,
Kpli and his people should go forward;
Let the white man's guns boom,
We are marching forward;
We all shall sleep in calico.

When we start, the ground shall shake;
The war is within our very huts;
Cowards should fall back
And live at home with the women;
They who go near our wives
While we are away in battle
Shall lose their calabashes when we come.

Where has it been heard before
That a snake has bitten a child
In front of its own mother;
The war is upon us
It is within our very huts
And the sons of men shall fight it
Let the white man's guns boom
And its smoke cover us
We are fighting them to die.

We shall die on the battlefield
We shall like death at no other place,
Our guns shall die with us
And our sharp knives shall perish with us
We shall die on the battlefield.

The Sea Eats the Land at Home

At home the sea is in the town,
Running in and out of the cooking places,
Collecting the firewood from the hearths
And sending it back at night;
The sea eats the land at home.
It came one day at the dead of night,
Destroying the cement walls,
And carried away the fowls,
The cooking-pots and the ladles,
The sea eats the land at home;
It is a sad thing to hear the wails,
And the mourning shouts of the women,
Calling on all the gods they worship,
To protect them from the angry sea.
Aku stood outside where her cooking-pot stood,
With her two children shivering from the cold,
Her hands on her breast,
Weeping mournfully.
Her ancestors have neglected her,
Her gods have deserted her,
It was a cold Sunday morning,
The storm was raging,
Goats and fowls were struggling in the water,
The angry water of the cruel sea;
The lap-lapping of the bark water at the shore,
And above the sobs and the deep and low moans,
Was the eternal hum of the living sea.
It has taken away their belongings
Adena has lost the trinkets which
Were her dowry and her joy,
In the sea that eats the land at home,
Eats the whole land at home.

Three poems from *Rediscovery* (1964)

Lovers' Song

Call her, call her for me, that girl
That girl with the neck like a desert tree
Call her that she and I will lie in one bed.
When you went away
Isn't it seven years?
Shall I fold mine and say I am cheap
Returned unsold from the market
If they marry a woman don't they sleep with her?
Isn't it seven years now since you went away?

The Weaver Bird

The weaver bird built in our house
And laid its eggs on our only tree
We did not want to send it away
We watched the building of the nest
And supervised the egg-laying.
And the weaver returned in the guise of the owner
Preaching salvation to us that owned the house
They say it came from the west
Where the storms at sea had felled the gulls
And the fishers dried their nets by lantern light
Its sermon is the divination of ourselves
And our new horizons limit at its nest
But we cannot join the prayers and answers of the communicants.
We look for new homes every day,
For new altars we strive to rebuild
The old shrines defiled by the weaver's excrement.

Easter Dawn

That man died in Jerusalem
And his death demands dawn marchers
From year to year to the sound of bells.
The hymns flow through the mornings
Heard on Calvary this dawn.
    the gods are crying, my father's gods are crying
    for a burial – for a final ritual –
    but they that should build the fallen shrines
    have joined the dawn marchers
    singing their way towards Gethsemane
    where the tear drops of agony still freshen the cactus.
He has risen! Christ has risen!
    the gods cried again from the hut in me
    asking why that prostration has gone unheeded.
The marchers sang of the resurrection
That concerned the hillock of Calvary
Where the ground at the foot of the cross is level.
    the gods cried, shedding
    clayey tears on the calico
    the drink offering had dried up in the harmattan
    the cola-nut is shrivelled
    the yam feast has been eaten by mice
    and the fetish priest is dressing for the Easter service.
The resurrection hymns come to me from afar
touching my insides.
    Then the gods cried loudest
    Challenging the hymners.
    They seized their gongs and drums
    And marched behind the dawn marchers
    Seeking their Calvary
    Seeking their tombstones
    And those who refused to replace them
    In the appropriate season.

From *Night of My Blood* (1971)

At the Gates

I do not know which god sent me,
to fall in the river
and fall in the fire.
These have failed.
I move into the gates
demanding which war it is;
which war it is?
the dwellers in the gates
answer us; we will let that war come
they whom we followed to come
sons of our own mothers and fathers
bearing upon our heads nothing
save the thunder that does roar
who knows when evil matters will come.

Open the gates!
It is Akpabli Horsu who sent me
Open the gates, my mother's children
and let me enter
our thunder initiates have run amok
and we sleep in the desert land
not moving our feet
we will sleep in the desert
guns in our hands we cannot fire
knives in our hands we cannot throw
the death of a man is not far away.

I will drink it; it is my god who gave it to me
I will drink this calabash
for it is god's gift to me
bachelor, never go too far
for the drummer boys will cook and let you eat.

Don't cry for me
my daughter, death called her
it is an offering of my heart
the ram has not come to stay
three days and it has gone
elders and chiefs whom will I trust
a snake has bitten my daughter
whom will I trust?
walk on gently; give me an offering
that I will give it to God
and he will be happy.

Uproot the yams you planted
for everything comes from God
it is an evil god who sent me
that all I have done
I bear the magic of the singer that has come
I have no paddle, my wish,
to push my boat into the river.

From *Ride Me, Memory* (1973)

Afro-American Beats III: An American Memory of Africa

Black as my night, anonymous here
my death in Elizabethville was your death.
Blood shed in Sharpeville was shed before in Ulundi
Alabama, Memphis
Fred Hampton on a Chicago bed
blood and gun fire in darkness
was it prophesied that the panther
shall die in his bed without a leap?
I hug my black skin here against my better judgement
hung my shields and sheaves for a season

Leaving Africa that September 1967
in flight from the dreams we build
in the pale talons of eagles yard
donkeys braying on the bloody field across the square
the bulge of my sails unfurl for the
harbour of hate;
The pride of this colour
by which they insist on defining my objection;
that I am a nigger is no matter
but that I died in Memphis and Elizabethville
outrages my self-esteem
I plot my vengeance silently
like Ellison's men in bright dens
of hiding and desperate anonymity
and with the hurricanes and eagles of tomorrow
prepare a firm and final rebuttal to your lies.
To be delivered in the season of infinite madness.

From *The House by the Sea* (1978)

The First Circle

1

   the flat end of sorrow here
two crows fighting over New Year's Party
leftovers. From my cell, I see a cold
        hard world.

2

So this is the abscess that
    hurts the nation –
      jails, torture, blood
        and hunger.
  One day it will burst;
      it must burst.

3

When I heard you were taken
we speculated, those of us at large
where you would be
in what nightmare will you star?
That night I heard the moans
wondering whose child could now
be lost in the cellars of oppression.
Then you emerged, tall, and bloody-eyed.

It was the first time
        I wept.

4

        The long nights I dread most
          the voices from behind the bars
        the early glow of dawn before
the guard's steps wake me up,
the desire to leap and stretch
and yawn in anticipation
of another dark home-coming day
only to find that
        I cannot.
        riding the car into town
hemmed in between them
        their guns poking me in the ribs,
        I never had known that my people
        wore such sad faces, so sad
        they were on New Year's Eve,
        so very sad.

From *Collected Poems* (1987)

Had Death Not Had Me in Tears

Had death not had me in tears
I would have seen the barges
on life's stream sail.
I would have heard sorrow songs
in groves where the road was lost
long
where men foot prints mix with other men foot prints
By the road I wait
'death is better, death is better'
came the song
I am by the roadside
looking for the road
death is better, death is much better
Had death not had me in tears
I would have seen the barges
I would have found the road
and heard the sorrow songs.
The land wreathes in rhythm
with your soul, caressed by history
and cruel geography
landscape ineffable yet screaming
eloquent resonance like the drums
of after harvests.
We pile rocks on terracing love
Carry the pithy cloth
to cover the hearths of our mother.

Come now, you lucky ones
come to the festival of corn and lamb
to the finest feast of this land
come, now,

your lovers have unfurled
their clothes
their thighs glistening like golden knives
ready for the plunging,
for the plentiful loving time.
To whom shall I turn
to what shall I tell my woes?
My kinsmen, the desert tree
denied us sustenance
long before the drought.
To whom shall I turn
to whom shall I tell my woes?
Some say tell the mother goat
she too is kinswoman
elemental sister of your clan
But I cannot tell the mother goat
for she is not here.

Ayi Kwei Armah

Seed Time

To the hot-eyed hustler urging speed
over preparation, saying
knowledge of self yea
probing the universe fine
digging connections in between sure
but the rev is urgent work and
there's no time now, right? Say
wrong.
Say preparation is
time spent, not wasted.
Add the image:
Ra took ages
still hasn't finished:
all history is foreplay.
Should the hustler counter, teasing:
Shoot, but this your Ra's unreal
mystic stuff, say
no my love
agreed,
reality includes prestressed concrete
bullets, nitroglycerine
rustproof steel and lasers
but that's hardly all
unless you think
your intellect
unreal.
Say
Ra's a mythic paradigm

but
what are myths and
paradigms
but psychic feet and hands projected
through the universe
to help us move
from what happened to us
to what we need to be? Say
no my love
Ra's no self-created god
Ra is our self-creation
Ra is us
embracing space
traversing time. So
no my love
whatever we've run short of
this hasty day
its name cannot be
time.

News

Yesterday
there was another attempted
coup.
People are still running blind
targeting the latest scapeleaders
in the game of
neocolonial chairs
grooming more aching psyches
to play redeemer
trying individual cures for
social cancers

they keep straining to slash apart
the current ruling knot
in what they hope to call
a relatively bloodless
coup
they dream of substituting
another small tight group
for the one serving its bitter time
at the tip of
the overripe colonial abscess
on this sliver of our continental home
we've been conned into calling
our state.

Ama Ata Aidoo

Totems

I
came upon an owl
at the crossroads
blinking with confusion
greater than
mine!

Bird of doom.
Bird of promise.

Fluorescent lightning on a
city corn-field,
tell the owl of
the changing times.

They-of-the-Crow
cannot
carve out
destinies through
marriage.

Whoever can?

He does
too well by her,
                              and
she always
knows when
starched rags go to swaddle
another's baby.

Dodua of the light palms:
She is hanging out the
last new to dry from its
first washing.

Perch where you can, and
tell your story. They make
us believe that all roofs
cover homes from the rain.

Akua my sister,
No one chooses to stand
under a tree in a storm.

So
You
shall not be the one to remind
Me
to keen for the great ancestors and
call to mind the ruined hamlet
that was once
the Home of Kings.

*Itu kwan
ma
Adze sa wo aa
na
Adze asa wo!!!*

Atukwei Okai

999 Smiles
(to Guy Warren)

nine hundred and ninety-nine smiles
plus
one quarrel ago, our eyes and our
hearts
were in agreement full that still

The sun rises in the East
And sets in the West, that
Still
Rains fall from above
Downward to the earth
That
Still smokes rise from the
Earth, reaching for the sky
That
Still our earth is round and
Not flat like a spread-out
Mat

and yet . . .
      see where
            today
you have
    gone
        to sit . . .
throwing . . .
      stones
         at us . . .

poisonous . . .
        stones
           at us . . .
satanic . . .
       stones . . .
            at us . . .

And if I still had my hands
On my shoulders I should raise
One of my hands above my
Head
And gauge and catch your
Stones, one by one, while they
Were still hot in the cool
Air,

and yet . . .
      see where . . .
               today
you have
     gone
         to sit . . .
hurling . . .
      stones . . .
          at us . . .
hurling . . .
      stones . . .
          at us . . .
infernal . . .
       stones . . .
           at us . . .
sinister . . .
      stones . . .
          at us . . .

But all the same, I shall not even
Utter your name, lest the fast and
Faithful

Winds repeat it to the hearing of
Our ancestors who are asleep
With
Their eyes, but not asleep with
Their ears, lest our ancestors
Angrily
Rise out of their nest and
Breathe out the winds that can
Shake
Till it breaks, the decayed drooping
Branch
upon which
        of all
            people
you today
      have gone
           to sit . . .
hurling . . .
      stones . . .
           at us . . .
wrathful . . .
      stones . . .
           at us . . .
saddening . . .
      stones . . .
           at us . . .

Charging precisely to our
Head, and if I still had my
Hands about me, I would
Gather
Your stones into a heap, and
Leave them there to lie till
Some morrow when we might
Use

Them to bring down to the warm
Tongues of some fire, fleshy
Birds, that above our heads are

Perched,
Just like you, upon the slippery
Branch of the air; and if still
I had my hands with me, I would
Catch
And keep your stones without thinking
Of throwing them back at you – but
The hands too soon you have stolen away
With
you
    to where
            today
you have
        gone
            to perch
throwing . . .
        stones . . .
                at us . . .
venomous . . .
        stones . . .
                at us . . .
spiteful . . .
        stones . . .
                at us . . .

nine hundred and ninety-nine smiles
plus
one quarrel ago our eyes and our
hearts
were in agreement full that still

When a man lifts his foot, it is
Forward
That he places it, that still, each
Human
Being owns only ten fingers on two
Hands

Kojo Laing

Black Girl, White Girl

Ampa I used to walk through the streets
with a black girl and a white girl
and they both looked exactly alike:
high cheekbones, slimmish, good hair, calm,
and with a fine sense of history.

I used to walk through the streets ampa
with a white girl and a black girl,
exactly alike they both looked:
calm, slimmish, good hair, high cheekbones,
and with a fine sense of history.

Slimmish, high cheekbones, good hair, calm,
a black girl and a white girl
who both looked exactly alike,
used to walk ampa through the streets with me,
with my terrible sense of history.

Me in the high streets, my cheek with bruised bones,
me looking exactly like my history,
slim enough to push eternity forward, calm
with vaseline in my hair, good for all colours.

They ask: Why did you walk through the streets
with a black girl and a white girl,
both looking exactly alike,
good hair, calm, slimmish, high cheekbones?

I said: Check your history!
Check the omelettes, the light-soup, the mixed grill,
  the ampesi,
    Check the high cheekbones,
        the slimmish, the good, the hair, the calm.
    Check possibly love, Love!

Godhorse

The horse with birds on its mane, doubt on its tail . . .
doubt about the flies being whisked north or south . . .
crawled out of the relieved horizon, in
a burst of dung part-coloured with kente.
And the angle at which the horse bisected the hills,
made it easy for the old man with the square body
to jump up its decorated left flank, leaving
half his age behind as his bones came down like a pounder.
Galloping was a definition of time, more
for the man, less for the horse
whose high brown snorting would be framed
if only there were strong hands,
if only the ancestors would jump the centuries.
Now a woman raised her right breast on the right flank
of this horse of wonder, this horse
with a mane maimed by the limiting beauty of birds.
Mansa's whole body shook – O god of soft thunder! –
as the old man stretched his lust across horse flesh,
trying to speed through the geography of tails, but
suddenly meeting ghana
                        half-way up the horse instead; suddenly
seeing bishops and fetish priests
so that his reverence gently covered his lust, true
the religious men wanted to bless the impudent hooves, but
the horse threw off angels with a burst of shank, with
the old man kneeling on the saddle and begging Mansa for love,
as her breasts shook in incense.

Since the sun and moon were
                    in a simultaneous sky,
Mansa watched half a country hang on half a horse,
                    watched the old man's smiles and rejected each
                              one,
throwing the most outrageous one under the hardest hoof.
Pound your laughter, pound your world!
Rejection was no different, even when mixed with speed,
old man's nails were digging into horse country,
old man's knees were shaking the shanks
                    of a suddenly stationary stallion:
horse hair was full of brown regret,
                    was full of the morality of not galloping
when the country was sagging with the speed of time.
But let horse dung salute accra!
Let the blue moon burst over a clear gallop!
Let them rise against the unwanted pity of horse ethics!
We want the african touch, neighed the horse, for
it desperately loved Mansa's thighs pressing against it. But
old man shouted the horse on. Onnnn!
For the half of ghana that was missing
                    was merely the gaps in his old teeth,
                    was merely the spatial side of galloping.
On! Human flesh orbits horse flesh!
Old man falls from flank to flank,
bouncing across a withering country, shivering
under the weight of horse decrees
                    that Mansa carried on behalf of the authorities.
On! with the most moral horse in the world, for its
thighs did not return the pressure of Mansa's thighs, for
after all the universe was a stilled gallop,
                    was an old man crawling away from a cantering,
                              crazy life,
                    was a contradictory shank shaking.
As Mansa fell off at last by the tune of a distant highlife,
the horse snorted for other women, the
    horse . . . its morality lost in its speed at last . . .
                    threw off the old man.

Man, poor, old: he died with a smile before he hit the ground:
>   and under him were the crushed birds, O God,
>   carrying their expanding beauty still, still.

I am the Freshly Dead Husband

I am the freshly dead husband,
I write my death to a fashionable wife:
Dear Dede with the new-bought guarantees, Dede
with the obsession to push hurriedly some
shared memories into my crowded box, crowded
with the two parts of me that were still alive:
> brain and popylonkwe
>   still vibrant above the desolation of my other parts,
>   above the rotting of my stylish wrists.
I was not properly dead,
I could hear you chat prettily as I lay in state . . .
>   and what a state, involving an accident
>   with a supertobolo girlfriend still alive . . .
with a funeral cloth of the best style, paid
from the breathless anticipation of my retiring benefits.
Boxes and benefits, hearts and betrayal, ginnnnn!
>   How can you mourn me!
To shed tears you had to borrow
from the sorrow of your father's funeral
held last year, when I couldn't cry.
Together my actions and your inventions pushed
all grief to the children who,
not knowing any better, loved my carefree syncopations.
Dede with the black-brown eyes
>   whose shades were deeper in the left eye, I
salute your show of courageous grief when
you convinced my mother of the authenticity of your tears!
Bless you, your grief was becoming so successful
that you were, with decorum, fantastically enjoying my death.
I am dead but hungry for guavas . . .

I foolishly imagined the rainbow,

                           with its inappropriate joy,

torn from a sky that never gave me any sign till I was dead.

Dede, don't let them push my hearse so fast, have

a little posthumous consideration

                   for my erection of the after-life:

a dead man can't go to God with his popylonkwe at attention.

God forgive your speed

for you want to disgrace me before the ancestors!

Hurrying to bury me . . .

hey wait, the erection still stands . . .

was the horror for my mother, whose

tears, so bewildered, could not quite reach me

                     in my wooden flagless castle . . . she

was beginning to sense a picnic atmosphere,

demure girls danced in their walk by my grey skin

              now spiritual at last, at last.

                  And I wish my funeral would panic!

Dede I agree I often betrayed you, usually

just at the point when you were

                  simultaneously betraying me, I

imprisoned you in my successes and excesses,

I took your gin and doubled it.

As I speak these words,

fresh ants crawl over me with their white eggs, I

noiselessly knock and bite my coffin! for

it is too tight for me to wear, I need a different size!

Dede, help me, I demand air-conditioning, I need

the coolness now that you never gave me! But

your back is turned, you adjust your duku in the mirror.

You look in great fashion by my rotting chin.

Did you really have to try so hard

to stop yourself from laughing, as

you realized that I was dreaming

about being buried next to that girl that I REALLY loved!??

And she did burst out laughing as the last dust covered me . . .
And her laughter said: I was truthful about all my boxed lies.
Yes, but I will write again!
I see the ginnnnn of resurrection glass to glass!

And she did burst out laughing as she had then entered me
And her laughter said: I was fearful about . . .
Yes, but I will write again.
I see the portrait of resurrection glass in glass!

Kofi Anyidoho

Hero and Thief

I was counting time in the heartbeat of the storm
when Fui and Eɲyo came riding through whirlwinds
she with the dream beauty of new rainbows
and he in his quiet way spoke of how
a nervous govt sits on a bankrupt stool
wearing a gown of fantasy and hope
telling tales of foreign aid and godmothers at Christmas time

Is it enough we search the private dreams of poets
when our land's nightmares give birth to strange desires
and our children draw their wishes in the quicksands of this earth?
Is it enough is it enough we probe the pampered dreams of poets
while our people scratch the dunghills of this earth
where once the flowers bloomed and poured perfume
upon the pestilence of rotten memories?
Is it enough is it enough we dream in foreign languages
and drink champagne in banquet halls of a proud people
while our people crack palm kernels with their teeth?
It is not enough it isn't enough
to go in search of the lone hero
while the common thief inherits our ancient stools

There have been thieves before on our land

when the harvest left enough surplus for the thieving hand
and we said the thief never reaps much more than farm owner
But the harvest dance is gone
Our harvest gatherers crawl on empty granary floors
keeping tears away with ancient festive hopes:

my people, how soon again in our hive shall we swarm around
    our
      honey-comb?

So the thieving hand has reaped much more than farm owner
and the harvest dream transforms into slow funereal hopes
the rice harvest has gone to weaverbird
the corn-on-the-cob has gone to grasscutter
the yam-in-the-mound was carried off by rat
and now we sit and watch the flowering bean and
the ripened fruit of palm being plucked at dawn
by slippery hands of night workers

Tomorrow at noon we'll flock the conference hall
of the academy of sciences and hear the learned talk
on post-harvest perspiration of yam tubers
    Is it enough is it enough to dream the moon and stars
    When this earth we own we can't possess?

Soul in Birthwaters

vi. *Ghosts*

a thousand ghosts haunt our soul in birth waters
this life would drown in blood
hammer falls on anvil of
this head, calabash cracks
scattering braindrops on pathways
offering a broken tale to passers-by

watch revolutions of worlds
load guts of goats with power of
bulls, the fools we were
we would seek refuge on wings of their visions
deserting the dream we placed among the thorns

they stole our sleep in a daylight siege
and in our brief madness we
exchanged lullabies for anguished cries

we were all away on the farm
when prowlers of night
snaked into our pillows
oh they would ambush our sleep
and strangle our dream
the vampires! I saw them
they know I saw them when
father sent me home to fetch a little salt

My voice my voice they seek after my voice!
Do not put me to sleep my people.

A Dirge for Our Birth

Let us not ignore the testimony
        of our own misdeeds
and impair our reasoning with
        a stupid reliance on prophecies
        of these new Seers

In the early days of the craze
        for negation of our Past
did we not buy a coffin and celebrate the burial
        of a Brother who still walked
        this Earth with us?
did we not burn his barn   and allow a clown
        to rape his wife
        before our very eyes?

What fate befell the Child implanted in her womb?
Did we not refuse to attend the ceremony of his Birth?
And when he died   so young   of *kwasbiorkor*
        how many wept for him?

Who can tell where they are today?
       the old priestess
          who read our future in a calabash
       the unhappy poet
          who composed a dirge for the ceremony of our Birth?
Did we not twist their jaws and drive them

       beyond the boundaries of our dreams?

Now we ask our mothers to confirm
       the things our grandmothers say.
We beg our children to tell us who we were.

Sound and Silence

Because   because I do not scream
You do not know how bad I hurt

Because   because I do not kiss
          on public squares
You may not know how much I love

Because   because I do not swear
          again and again and again
You wouldn't know how deep I care

You keep saying
How somehow our world must live by signs
But see how much we give away
Doing time in pursuit of signs
    deprived of all meaning
       and of all purpose
We break our words in two. Then we
Split each half into sounds and silences

Guinea

Ahmed Tidjani-Cissé

Home News

'My dear son I am well thanks be to God
I pray for you day and night.'

'My dear brother it's my sad duty to announce
the death of our beloved mother
Which occurred last Sunday
after a short illness.'

'My cousin I've grown a lot
send me some trousers and new shoes.'

'My love, it's now ten years I've been awaiting you
What's keeping you there in the white man's land
think of the trouble you cause us
by such a long absence.'

'My dear friend our country's changing
into a huge shanty-town.
No one can eat his fill except . . .
Send me a tape-recorder.'

'My dear son it is I your father
I beg you to return to your land
if not you will not have even
the sorrow of recognizing my tomb.'

'My dear nephew, I must tell you
of your father's death
we all hope you'll be able to attend
the forty-days' wake.'

'My dear . . .'
A tear yesterday when the postman passed
Anxiety today in awaiting his return
The abyss of sadness envelops me
When I have no news from home.
My soul shrivels a little
When home news tumbles over me.
The other day I made a fleeting boat
Full of home news.
I set it in the water at the wharf of Exile-Overseas.
I went to attend its arrival
at the landing stage of Loneliness-under-Hope.
My boat landed some secret passengers for me
Next day the postman's prophetic hand was
stretched towards me.

'My dear friend, your brother was arrested
last week in reprisal
for your political work against the government
Your family is left without a head
Send me a shirt and a neck-tie.'

Of Colours and Shadows

Royal blue azure blue
The nobility of a colour
to clothe the uncertainty of conditions.
Green-blue turquoise blue
The adornments of nature
scorn the audacities of imitation
they ornament the fleeting hair of the tornado.
Ash grey, dirty grey, iron grey, pearl grey
The metamorphosing power of a colour
which shatters the yokes of comparison.
Sulphur yellow, saffron yellow, golden yellow
Fever can be yellow
Yellow is a self-respecting colour

The yellow of the egg was the beginning
But the respect for a colour is only apparent
when the yellow peril is in question.
Vermilion red, blood red, poppy red
Cardinals' purple is a red
which sends howling the Gehenna of fear.
The purple of Caesars is all-conquering
Cortez and Pizarro have flaunted the colours of Europe
to the redskins in organizing a hecatomb.
Marxism-Leninism is red
There are colours of poverty
fetishist colours
opulent colours
colours which strike terror or which the whole world unfurls.
Milk white kapok white
The moon is white
Innocence is white
the blindman's stick is white
the Ku-Klux-Klan is robed in white
my village was evangelized by the White Fathers.
Their words were transmitted with the aid of white cold steel.
To fashion the centuries of history
men have invented all the nuances of a colour.
Black bread, black night, black misery
Mourning is black, the devil is black
with black ebony one can construct
a black market to supply the fields
with cotton of the whitest fibre.
The colours which compose my rainbow
Have the density of shadows.
At the borders of my rainbow
history has allowed only a clear obscurity to float.
Like a raging cataract
the dusky shadows of my colour
make a rampart around my house
every time I try to break
the barriers of colour.
Red, blue, yellow, white, black.

The shadows of colours are not truly multicoloured.
Red as palm oil
The snow hides in its own whiteness
behind my door
it will not see me
I have ceased to be the shadow of my colour.

Kenya

Khadambi Asalache

Death of a Chief

pavements lined
sorrowful silence
tears
the coffin off to somewhere
in black
behind it the entire district
involved
in songs of grief
that flow and follow
a trailing gesture
thoughts
battered syllables
on lips

as past periods
return
in the farewell
of the blank faces
to float a fable
dreams
years of his reign

the path is silent
to this procession
walking into a myth
as he passes
alone
freed from praises
the worldly notion
the sensate achievement that floats

on tongues like a wind
like changeable news

this slow walk seems
a readjustment
from his life
a transit
a sampling of the fragrance
of death and the surprise of
its calm
an eternal grip
cold

Jonathan Kariara

A Leopard Lives in a Muu Tree

A leopard lives in a Muu tree
Watching my home
My lambs are born speckled
My wives tie their skirts tight
And turn away –
Fearing mottled offspring.
They bathe when the moon is high
Soft and fecund
Splash cold mountain stream water on their nipples
Drop their skin skirts and call obscenities.
I'm besieged
I shall have to cut down the Muu tree
I'm besieged
I walk about stiff
Stroking my loins.
A leopard lives outside my homestead
Watching my women
I have called him elder, the one-from-the-same-womb
He peers at me with slit eyes
His head held high
My sword has rusted in the scabbard.
My wives purse their lips
When owls call for mating
I'm besieged
They fetch cold mountain water
They crush the sugar cane
But refuse to touch my beer horn.
My fences are broken
My medicine bags torn

The hair on my loins is singed
The upright post at the gate has fallen
My women are frisky
The leopard arches over my homestead
Eats my lambs
Resuscitating himself.

Jared Angira

If

a squirrel crosses my way
while on a trip
then luck is mine
but when it's a cheetah
or wild cat that crosses there
I turn and go back.

I knock my right foot on stone
while on a trip
I melt in joy
since I shall be overfed
but when it's the left
I turn and go back.

I slip in my shirt
the inside coming out
I jump in merriment
for I shall be overfed.

the first being
I meet in the feeble dawn
is an old woman
I turn to my blanket
it's all ill luck

I dream my relative dead
in midst of sweet slumbers
I wake in joy
knowing he's overfed
the previous night

and if I dream I am dead
I rejoice
for growing an inch.
and if I dream
of my ideal girl
then I lose hope
the answer is no.

I wake up in the morning
and find my teeth shaking
and loose
surely I know
they went eating excreta
while soul courted in fairyland.

A hen crows
it must be killed
bad omen
a dog howls
instead of barking
the village owner
is at death's door
and if I walk on my head
then I am dead.

The Country of the Dead

The country of the dead
I speak
no answer
I weep
no pity
I watch
no colour
I listen
no sound
the country of the dead

I shout, the echo strikes
the dead rock
I kick, my toe mutilates
on dry stump
I weep, no pity
the country of the dead

I've searched the exit
but heard no owls
no parrots, the waves beat afar
on wrecks of ships
the sand stares with me
the country of the dead.

Manna

So all waited for manna
In the orange dawn
And let their feet
Crack in the dew

No one bothered to ask
The labourers
To bring forth this manna

Many said
A miracle recorded
For God never laboured

The first shipment
Of this manna
Landed to a clean swept spot
And many wide throated waiters
Never chanced to see it.

Children wailed in hunger
Idle mothers rushed
To the screening chamber

Even mothers
Who had worked
Mighty hard
Sank in the scrum

Soon the manna craft
Took off from ground
And hungry natives
Soared the sky
But they only saw
The rainbow
Which promised them
Hunger in seven days
Death in seven ways.

A Look in the Past

Once I was a lizard
cheeky and harmless
and built clouds
that the heat
never could melt

I learnt
of the transanimation
into a monitor
deaf to all spikes
a dweller of two worlds . . .

ere my breath had settled
my back grew rough –
my teeth went chisel-like
. . . a crocodile
lurking in sandy seafloor

then one day I died
but knocked my head
on the sharp gravestone
that woke me up
to find me winged
tough-clawed and a scavenger . . .
I was an eagle.

I went on sojourn
and my red eyes blue'ed
till I turned priestly –
pigeoned
till we came to Guernica
where they pinched my olive branch
and gave me a bone

when next I stopped
I was gliding
mutilated . . .
the mongoose pursued me in hideways

I shall go back
to the formless clouds
and melt myself into rain
then shall I land in the plantation
and mate with the secondary roots
of the old fig tree.

Request

Open your palms
to form a jar
and pour there water
to quench the thirst

Open your throat
and form a fan
to blow it over
and cool the panting soul

Burst open the gates
of that home
where Jove
lies in majesty
of loneliness

Tear off the curtain
of the window
on the facade
of satisfaction
and pass me through
to the honeyed comb

Open your bosom
and release
the juice
denied a seedling
below the brassieres

Coil your tongue
Aloo
Aloo
ignite your yellow breath
and let me pass
to the honeyed comb.

Micere Githae Mugo

I Want You to Know

I want you to know
how carefully
I watered the tender shoots
you planted
in my little garden.

Flowers now adorn the ground
the fruits are ripe
Come
bring a strongly woven basket
and bring with you also
the finest palm wine
that your expert tapping
can brew
we must feast and wine
till the small hours
of our short days together

Joy and love
shall be our daily
harvest songs.

Wife of the Husband

His snores
protect the sleeping hut
but the day's
load

and the morrow's
burden
weigh heavily over
the stooping mother as she

sweeps the hut
bolts the pen
tidies the hearth
buries the red charcoals
and finally seeks
her restless bed

His snores
welcome her to bed
four hours to sunrise
His snores rouse her from bed
six sharp
Arise
O, wife of the husband!

Marina Gashe

The Village

Kanyariri, Village of Toil,
Village of unending work.
Like a never dying spring,
Old women dark and bent
Trudge along with their hoes
To plots of weedy maize.
Young wives with donkeys
From cockcrow to setting of the sun
Go about their timeless duties,
Their scraggy figures like bows set in a row,
Plod up and down the rolling village farms
With loads on their backs
And babies tied to their bellies.
In the fields all day they toil
Stirring up the soil with hands and knives
Like chickens looking for worms.
Nothing here seems to sit still.
Even the village church is like a favourite well
Where the 'Revivalists' with their loudspeakers
Never cease calling people
To confess their sins and drink the Water of Life.
At dawn men ride away leaving the womenfolk
To fend for the bony goats and the crying children.

Maina wa Kinyatti

The Bride

The smell of the toilet bucket was sharp
The air in the cell was boiling hot
My body was bathing in sweat
I woke up in disgust

The man at the corner was having
An affair with his new bride
He threw a cold stare at me
The long imprisonment has unhinged him
Somewhat

Interrupted
They could not continue
The husband dismounted
The bride remained calm

Ashamed to look at me

The silence continued
Then both of them were deeply asleep
Their arms locked around each other
The couple in love
Strange love
But from what human depths was it born?
From what chamber of the body does it spring?
I wondered . . . I wondered
I could not sleep for a long time

3 October 1983
Kamiti M. S. Prison

Madagascar

Jean-Joseph Rabéarivelo

Four poems from *Traduits de la nuit*

2

What invisible rat
come from the walls of night
gnaws at the milky cake of the moon?
Tomorrow morning,
when it has gone,
there will be bleeding marks of teeth.

Tomorrow morning
those who have drunk all night
and those who have abandoned their cards,
blinking at the moon
will stammer out:
'Whose is that sixpence
that rolls over the green table?'
'Ah!' one of them will add,
'our friend has lost everything
and killed himself!'

And all will snigger
and, staggering, will fall.
The moon will no longer be there:
the rat will have carried her into his hole.

3

The hide of the black cow is stretched,
stretched but not set to dry,
stretched in the sevenfold shadow.

But who has killed the black cow,
dead without having lowed, dead without having roared,
dead without having once been chased
over that prairie flowered with stars?

She who calves in the far half of the sky.

Stretched is the hide
on the sounding-box of the wind
that is sculptured by the spirits of sleep.

And the drum is ready
when the new-born calf,
her horns crowned with spear grass
leaps
and grazes the grass of the hills.

It reverberates there
and its incantations will become dreams
until the moment when the black cow lives again,
white and pink
before a river of light.

14

She
whose eyes are prisms of sleep
and whose lids are heavy with dreams,
she whose feet are planted in the sea
and whose shiny hands appear
full of corals and blocks of shining salt.

She will put them in little heaps beside a misty gulf
and sell them to naked sailors
whose tongues have been cut out,
until the rain begins to fall.

Then she will disappear
and we shall only see
her hair spread by the wind
like a bunch of seaweed unravelling,
and perhaps some tasteless grains of salt.

18

The black glassmaker
whose countless eyeballs none has ever seen,
whose shoulders none has overlooked,
that slave all clothed in pearls of glass,
who is strong as Atlas
and who carries the seven skies on his head,
one would think that the vast river of clouds might carry him
    away,
the river in which his loincloth is already wet.

A thousand particles of glass
fall from his hands
but rebound towards his brow
shattered by the mountains
where the winds are born.

And you are witness of his daily suffering
and of his endless task;
you watch his thunder-riddled agony
until the battlements of the East re-echo
the conches of the sea –
but you pity him no more
and do not even remember that his sufferings begin again
each time the sun capsizes.

From *Presque-songes* (1934)

Cactus

That multitude of moulded hands
holding out flowers to the azure sky
that multitude of fingerless hands
unshaken by the wind
they say that a hidden source
wells from their untainted palms
they say that this inner source
refreshes thousands of cattle
and numberless tribes, wandering tribes
in the frontiers of the South.

Fingerless hands, springing from a source,
Moulded hands, crowning the sky.

Here, when the flanks of the City were still as green
as moonbeams glancing from the forests,
when they still left bare the hills of Iarive
crouching like bulls upthrust,
it was upon rocks too steep even for goats
that they hid, to protect their sources,
these lepers sprouting flowers.

Enter the cave from which they came
if you seek the origin of the sickness which ravages them –
origin more shrouded than the evening
and further than the dawn –
but you will know no more than I.
The blood of the earth, the sweat of the stone,
and the sperm of the wind,
which flow together in these palms
have melted their fingers
and replaced them with golden flowers.

I know a child, a prince in God's kingdom
Who would continue the tale:
'Fate took pity on the lepers
And told them to plant their flowers
And guard their springs afar from man's cruelty.'

Flavien Ranaivo

Song of a Young Girl

Oaf
the young man who lives down there
beside the threshing floor for rice;
like two banana-roots
on either side the village ditch,
we gaze on each other,
we are lovers,
but he won't marry me.
Jealous
his mistress I saw two days since at the wash house
coming down the path against the wind.
She was proud;
was it because she wore a lamba thick
and studded with coral
or because they are newly bedded?
However it isn't the storm
that will flatten the delicate reed,
nor the great sudden shower
at the passage of a cloud
that will startle out of his wits
the blue bull.
I am amazed;
the big sterile rock
survived the rain of the flood
and it's the fire that crackles
the bad grains of maize.
Such this famous smoker
who took tobacco
when there was no more hemp to burn.

A foot of hemp?
– Sprung in Andringitra,
spent in Ankaratra,
no more than cinders to us.
False flattery
stimulates love a little
but the blade has two edges;
why change what is natural?
– If I have made you sad
look at yourself in the water of repentance,
you will decipher there a word I have left.
Good-bye, whirling puzzle,
I give you my blessing:
wrestle with the crocodile,
here are your victuals and three water-lily flowers
for the way is long.

Song of a Common Lover

Don't love me, my dear,
like your shadow
for shadows fade at evening
and I want to keep you
right up to cockcrow;
nor like pepper
which makes the belly hot
for then I couldn't take you
when I'm hungry;
nor like a pillow
for we'd be together in the hours of sleep
but scarcely meet by day;
nor like rice
for once swallowed you think no more of it;
nor like soft speeches
for they quickly vanish;
nor like honey,

sweet indeed but too common.
Love me like a beautiful dream,
your life in the night,
my hope in the day;
like a piece of money,
ever with me on earth,
and for the great journey
a faithful comrade;
like a calabash:
intact, for drawing water;
in pieces, bridges for my guitar.

Malawi

David Rubadiri

An African Thunderstorm

From the west
Clouds come hurrying with the wind
Turning
Sharply
Here and there
Like a plague of locusts
Whirling
Tossing up things on its tail
Like a madman chasing nothing.

Pregnant clouds
Ride stately on its back
Gathering to perch on hills
Like dark sinister wings;
The Wind whistles by
And trees bend to let it pass.

In the village
Screams of delighted children
Toss and turn
In the din of whirling wind,
Women –
Babies clinging on their backs –
Dart about
In and out
Madly
The Wind whistles by
Whilst trees bend to let it pass.
Clothes wave like tattered flags
Flying off

To expose dangling breasts
As jaggered blinding flashes
Rumble, tremble, and crack
Amidst the smell of fired smoke
And the pelting march of the storm.

Felix Mnthali

My Father

That we may have life
and have it abundantly
he endured
the chrome-dust
the damp hell
of Selukwe Peak Mines
the pittance
of American multi-nationals –

They thought it was the watch
on which they had inscribed his name
'for a long and meritorious service'
that made him beam . . .
they never saw blacks
as men with ambition
but only as a 'labour force'
the long arm of their
'manifest destiny',
the vital source
of their strategic metals.

He smiled
   smiled because one day
   one day . . .
   his sons would return!

The Stranglehold of English Lit.
(for Molara Ogundipe-Leslie)

Those questions, sister,
those questions
                    stand
                    stab
                    jab
          and gore
too close to the centre!

For if we had asked
why Jane Austen's people
carouse all day
and do no work

would Europe in Africa
have stood
the test of time?
and would she still maul
the flower of our youth
in the south?
Would she?

Your elegance of deceit,
Jane Austen,
lulled the sons and daughters
of the dispossessed
into a calf-love
with irony and satire
around imaginary people.

While history went on mocking
the victims of branding irons
and sugar-plantations
that made Jane Austen's people
wealthy beyond compare!

Eng. Lit., my sister,
was more than a cruel joke –
it was the heart
of alien conquest.

How could questions be asked
at Makerere and Ibadan,
Dakar and Fort Hare –
with Jane Austen
at the centre?
How could they be answered?

The Celebration

Before bulging eyes
a cocoon breaks
and its worm spits
the venom of vipers!

Gliding kingfishers
muster
the fury of a hawk;
saplings and ferns brood
like baobabs in the Rift Valley;
from the back of nowhere
waifs prophesy
the day of judgement.

We have bedecked with flowers
gun-carriers, guns and bayonets;
filled gourds with honey
from mountains belching fire –

It is while it lasts,
the hour of revelation,
the well-spring of love and hate,
a celebration!

Jack Mapanje

Before Chilembwe Tree

1

Didn't you say we should trace
your footprints unmindful of
quagmires, thickets and rivers
until we reached your *nsolo* tree?

Now, here I seat my gourd of beer
on my little fire throw my millet
flour and my smoked meat while
I await the second coming.

2

Why does your mind boggle:
Who will offer another gourd
Who will force another step
To hide our shame?

The goat blood on the rocks
The smoke that issued
The drums you danced to
And the rains hoped for –

You've chanted yourselves hoarse
Chilembwe is gone in your dust
Stop lingering then:
Who will start another fire?

On Being Asked to Write a Poem for 1979

Without kings and warriors occasional verse fails

Skeletal Kampuchea children staring, cold
Stubborn Irish children throwing grenades
These are objects too serious for verse,
Crushed Soweto children clutching their entrails
Then in verse bruised, mocks

Today no poet sufficiently asks why dying children
Stare or throw bombs. And why should we
Compute painful doubts that will forever occupy us?
Talking oil-crises in our eight-cylinder cars
Is enough travesty . . .

The year of the child must make no difference then
Where tadpoles are never allowed to grow into frogs!

An Elegy for Mangochi Fishermen

Today even those fireflies have become
The banners for our night fishermen
The crabs and *dondolos* dare not
Peep out of their crevices.

The virgin canoe we once boasted about
Holding the head or pushing the rear
Pulling the lips or rolling on poles,
The canoe has capsized, the carvers drowned.

Those loin-cloths dripping, the muscles
Twitching with power, the husky voices chanting
About the delicious chambo dishes expected
Even the toes we once crushed dragging
Our canoe from the arid Namizimu mountains
To the soft beaches of this golden lake –

We will not cast in tender herbs to cure.
Today, you gone, the vigil wax has melted away
The light is out in our cryptic recesses
We must all lie in pitch dark stakes.

Should we then wipe our sticky brows
In the heat of another October? Should we fell
More poles to roll another canoe to the beach?
Is it worth it assembling another voice?

At the Metro: Old Irrelevant Images
(for Blaise)

They are still so anthropologically tall here
Still treating you in irrelevant tribal metaphors:
Somalis have softer skins, they drink milk; they say
(And yours is cracking, you drink *kachasu*!)

Even the most knowledgeable still slip back
Apologizing to you in banal Tarzan images:
The children still know mostly Tarzans at school; they say
(Tarzans choked me too in the fifties, damn it!)

But the College girls' sit-in about rapists was
A bit of a change, and Mrs Thatcher's et cetera
Against overseas students; and, the publisher's dinner!
(How are the jacarandas I left blooming, otherwise?)

The Cheerful Girls at Smiller's Bar, 1971

The prostitutes at Smiller's Bar beside the dusty road
Were only girls once in tremulous mini-skirts and oriental
Beads, cheerfully swigging Carlsbergs and bouncing to
Rusty simanje-manje and rumba booming in the juke-box.

They were striking virgins bored by our Presbyterian
Prudes until a true Presbyterian came one night. And like
To us all the girls offered him a seat on cheap planks
In the dark backyard room choked with diesel-oil clouds
From a tin-can lamp. Touched the official rolled his eyes
To one in style. She said no. Most girls only wanted
A husband to hook or the fruits of Independence to taste
But since then mini-skirts were banned and the girls
Of Smiller's Bar became 'ugly prostitutes to boot!'

Today the girls still giggle about what came through
The megaphones: the preservation of our traditional
et cetera . . .

The Famished Stubborn Ravens of Mikuyu

These could not be Noah's ravens, these crows
of Mikuyu Prison groaning on our roof-tops each
day; wherever they wandered after their bungled
pilgrimages in the aftermath of those timeless
floods, Noah's ravens could not have landed
here (they never returned to their master's ark).
These could not be Elijah's ravens either; for
however stubbornly this nation might challenge
Lord Almighty's frogs, these devouring locusts,
the endless droughts and plagues, today there's
no prophet God so loves as to want to rescue
(with the bread and meat from messenger ravens!).

These can only be from that heathen stock of
famished crows and carrion vultures sent here
to peck at our insomnia and agony-blood-eyes
and to club the peace of this desert cell with
their tough knocking beaks. And why don't they
choose some other place and some other time?

Why must these crows happen at Mikuyu Prison,
always at dawn, hammering at the corrugated
iron of this cell, drilling at the marrow of our
fragile bones and picking at the fishbones
thieved from the dustbins we ditched outside?

Your Tears Still Burn at My Handcuffs (1991)

After that millet beer you brewed, mother
(In case Kadango Mission made something of
Another lake-son for the village to strut

About!); and after that fury with Special
Branch when I was brought home handcuffed –
'How dare you scatter this peaceful house?

What has my son done? Take me instead, you
Insensitive men!' you challenged their threat
To imprison you too as you did not '*stop*

Your gibberish!' – After that constant care
Mother, I expected you to show me the rites
Of homing in of this political prisoner,

Perhaps with ground herbal roots dug by
Your hand and hoe, poured in some clay pot
Of warm water for me to suffuse, perhaps

With your usual wry smile about the herbs
You wish your mother had told you about.
Today, as I invent my own cleansing rites

At this return of another fugitive, without
Even dead roots to lean on, promise to bless
These lit candles I place on your head and

Your feet, accept these bended knees, this
Lone prayer offered among these tall unknown
Graveyard trees, this strange requiem mustered

From the tattered Catholic Choir of Dembo
Village. You gave up too early, mother: two
More months, and I'd have told you the story.

Of some Nchinji upstart who tamed a frog at
Mikuyu Prison, how he gave it liberty to invite
Fellow frogs to its wet niche, dearly feeding

Them insects and things; but how one day,
After demon bruises, his petulant inmate
Threw boiling water at the niche, killing

Frog and visitor. And I hoped you'd gather
Some tale for me too, one better than your
Granddaughter's about how you told her she

Would not find you on her return from school
That day. But we understand, after so many
Pointless sighs about your son's expected

Release, after the village ridicule of your
Rebellious breasts and sure fatigue of your
Fragile bones, your own minders, then your

Fear for us when the release did finally come –
You'd propose yet another exile, without you –
We understand you had to go, to leave us space

To move. Though now, among the gentle friends
Of these Jorvik walls, I wonder why I still
Glare at your tears burning at my handcuffs.

Smiller's Bar Revisited, 1983

No, how do you know they no longer seek what
Their hearts desire those girls at Smiller's Bar?

Note how they sneer at your dawns & bonfires now
That you have accidentalized* their beloved

Combatants. And having known so many nebulous
Fleas, why shouldn't they claim vague memories

Of your so-called liberation struggle? And in this
Feminist age, grant them revised metaphors, man!

You can't be so sure your buttercups gather here
Only to scent down the few rebels their masters

(Mindless-brittle-neck-hackers!) still invent
For them and what nonsense, what paranoia!

It's true at counters the masters lurch to your
Side, offering you round after round of beer,

Setting up their abandoned adulteresses for you
To settle on and enjoying their sadistic stories:

'That rhinoceros you gunned down scratching
His livid wounds on pepperwood, wasn't it fun

How he collapsed, twitching', they laugh hoping
You can join in the joke & be properly convicted!

But you must concede, after you accidentalized
Their Anenenjis, the nuance of your classical

Butterfly today slips away & even you don't know
Who the real master is when, from her creased

* accidentalize: to kill and pretend it was an accident when everybody knows it was
not (first used by the Writers Group, Chancellor College, University of Malawi,
1983/4).

Victorian frock, she rectifies your change without
Blush & pontificates about inflation having

Trebled her price. Indeed why should anybody's
Bastard at home eat grass? So, give the girls

A break, let the coloured bulbs, drunken moths
& robot drums choke the bay; who said freedom's

Not a bifurcated pig? Revisiting Smiller's Bar
May be the beginning of your true liberation!

Steve Chimombo

Napolo: The Message

Was it a decade after Napolo
I met you, friend?
No matter.
We lived to tell the story around the fire
in whispers and behind locked doors.
We are going to laugh together again
with empty mouths,
and dead eyes:
grimaces echoing hollowed minds.

Review what is left unsaid,
and, after we have parted,
we will know
what it is we wanted to say
before you noticed the dullness in my eyes
and I, the emptiness of your mouth,
before the art of saying nothing
in a mountain of words
interrupted our conversation.

In those days, my friend,
martyrs were left unburied,
heroes were coffined alive or fled.
Our tears remained unshed:
We did not know they had died.
No one told us who had gone.

These tears, my friend, are wrung
from a heart shattered
by the apocalypse
that was Napolo.

Developments from the Grave

1

We have come full circle,
it seems: burying our dead
right in the homestead now,
on the sites the living had built.

We no longer bury our corpses
over there and away from us,
overhung by weeping *nkhadzi* trees
just as the missionaries advised us.

We have come full circle,
at last: burying our dead
deep in the soil beneath us;
we climb over the mounds daily.

We no longer hang the cadavers
high in the trees away from scavengers:
hyenas, ants, beaks and talons;
just as the colonials instructed us.

2

We brought the dead to the homestead,
revived them as *ndondocha,**
cut off their tongues and tamed them
to live in our granaries for ever.

* *ndondocha*: zombies.

Bumper harvests come out of them
and we know who keeps the most,
organizing them into one task force
to labour in the tobacco, tea and cotton estates.

We unearthed the youth for *msendawana**
to skin them for their precious leather
and made purses out of the tender skin
for the most potent charm of them all.

We know who has the largest purse
accumulating wealth, and more.
Out of the mounds of our youth
sprout palaces, fleets and monuments.

3

Development did not catch us
by surprise, asleep or unprepared:
We knew about space exploration;
we had our own flying baskets.

The greenhouse effect is not news;
we know how to heat or cool the land:
Drought comes from a society on heat;
rain comes from a cooled nation.

But development came from the graves,
too full and closely packed to grow any more.
The protective *nkhadzi* trees fenced
each effort to force the grave boundaries.

We have now come full circle,
rightly so: living with our dead,
not only in *nsupa* or spirit houses
but in granaries, purses and coffins.

* *msendawana*: purses made of human skin.

Frank Chipasula

In a Free Country

They ran out of cuffs, but
with apologies for the inconvenience,
they carefully wrapped barbed wire
round the wrists of the political prisoners
who, as if in a ritual stretched
their arms out to the young masters.

The spikes strayed into the flesh still
and the prisoners marched, dancing as they
went into a little hut where all the free
people were herded and locked up like cattle;
The crimson prints marked the trail of tears
all the way to the camp, into the dark hut.

As they passed by the churches, the priests
closed their eyes and offered prayers for Muslims
and outsiders, calling them to Christ's salvation
and sang 'Bless our Messiah, long may he reign over us.'

The priests rode through the villages getting depleted,
determined to bring all heathens to the brotherhood.
They rode, skirting round the camp fences without
noticing the firm walls of metal thorns,
peering through the mesh, yet seeing no one.

They crossed their hearts for peace
as they passed mothers weeping inside their hearts
under the rough masks of laughter, for their
children dragged out of their bosoms,
chained like thieves and, like wild beasts,
kept inside the house of seven locks in solitary.

Those who were born to labour, to shred their muscles,
hummed sad songs as they turned out the soil,
tended the tobacco leaves, weeded the maize plants,
thinned the rice as blood-sucking worms stung
their weary feet in the waterlogged *dambos*.

Later, their masters received the coveted medals
from the highest authority in the land;
they were paraded around as master farmers
under showers of light bulbs and clicking shutters.

They too closed their ears to detainees' wails but
the swelling song of the plants as they ripened
under the groans of the labourers whose
children were made to dance under stinging whips.

On the radio, in the papers owned by the masters
we heard the story of our hard-earned freedom
repeated daily, hourly by the minute till our ears
gradually grew deaf and our sight impaired
by the daily flow of blood which the sun wept
and sought the cloth of the winds to dry it.

A Love Poem for My Country
for James

I have nothing to give you, but my anger
And the filaments of my hatred reach across the border
You, you have sold many and me to exile.
Now shorn of precious minds, you rely only on
What hands can grow to build your crumbling image.

Your streets are littered with handcuffed men
And the drums are thuds of the wardens' spiked boots.
You wriggle with agony as the terrible twins, law and order,
Call out the tune through the thick tunnel of barbed wire.

Here, week after week, the walls dissolve and are slim
The mist is clearing and we see you naked like
A body that is straining to find itself, but cannot
And our hearts thumping with pulses of desire or fear
And our dreams are charred chapters of your history.

My country, remember I neither blinked nor went to sleep
My country, I never let your life slide downhill
And passively watched you, like a recklessly driven car,
Hurrying to your crash while the driver leapt out.

The days have lost their song and salt
We feel bored without our free laughter and voice
Every day thinking the same and discarding our hopes.
Your days are loud with clanking cuffs
On men's arms as they are led away to decay.

I know a day will come and wash away my pain
And I will emerge from the night breaking into song
Like the sun, blowing out these evil stars.

Blantyre

Rusty grey roofs, stunted white-washed walls,
the city wears a borrowed Scottish accent,
and hides behind a clump of mango groves
and bluegums neighing like stray abandoned horses,
bathing, like shy maidens, in the early summer showers.

When the moon awoke, with bags under his eyes,
I knew the long vigil the night had kept in my mother's eyes
that had searched for her prodigal son far afield
in Timbuktu, my ancestral city, now unkempt, while

History stood still here as they shaved the city's head
with a blunt razor, broken bottles, leaving
tufts where red ants grazed with assegais and pen pistols:
Chilobwe still reeking blood, chaotic Ndirande stuck
in mud pools, Zimgwangwa shivering in the chill

Under the gaze of bungalows, mansions and palaces
built on plunder, ringed with barbed-wire fences
walled into personal prisons where fear rules.

The Rain Storm
for James

The rain washed the coat of the wind,
dusted the nose of the mountain,
licked the blood off its peak,
and rinsed the fish oils across the tarmac.

Here the road that had left us behind
stopped and waited for us, asked us
where we had been
when they skinned the land.

Then the road, braving the rain,
slithered between the mountains,
leaving us to marvel and to muse
where the thin tarmac was leading us.

And we wondered where the rain had been,
this rain that left drops of dreams
in our palms to sow in the soil of our hearts.

Under the eaves of the sky we set
Our open minds and filled them
With the purity that fell from heaven.

The Witch Doctor's Song

My people, beat the drums,
the male and female drums
that I may feed my famished feet

with the quickness of ancestral dance
and lay your bodies in the dust
that I may rest my soles on them.

Oh people of this village,
the whirlwind is coming
People of the village,
it uproots the banana groves.
The whirlwind is riding a hyena
and it is breaking your huts.

I will dance on the tail of the whirlwind:
the fool beats the drum, the wise ones dance.
My flywhisk bears me into every hut –
Beat the drums, people of this silent village;
who has died that you mourn in silence?
People of this dead village, tattoo me with your song.

The whirlwind has undressed the trees
Come and see, it has stripped this land bare
and it has stolen the best of our children;
The trees can no longer hide the heavy secrets:

When the river is in flood
it reaches the ankles
When the river is in flood
it reaches the ankles only.

The lake has stepped on a stone, hear its weeping;
The lake has scraped its foot on a sharp stone,

And beats its palms angrily on the sand like a drum
And the rain wearing colourful waist beads dances
The river floods your huts and loots your granaries

When the river is in flood
it reaches the ankles
When the river is in flood
it reaches the ankles only.

The sun has fallen, the whirlwind is rejoicing
under the village tree, wading through the flood.
The sun has fallen, beat the male and female drums.
The sun is sleeping, light a fire that I may feed
my thirsty feet with the sap of your song:

When the river is in flood
it reaches the ankles
When the river is in flood
it reaches the ankles only.

Nightfall
for Jack Mapanje

In the sad hotel that drinks a swamp,
You breathe malarial air and enjoy
Frog music piped in from the dismal swamp.

Bits of your life measured out in bars,
Your thoughts gripped in clamps,
Your lips pierced through

With fish-hooks, locked shut,
Silenced over the stab of a clipped
Tongue that stabs the steel bar clutching

The teeth gnashed for dinner.
You dunk salt balls into the soup
Of bitter tears raging through our land.

Fried cockroaches, rotten beans
Baked in the perennial salt
Whet your old ulcerous hunger

As you journey from nowhere to nowhere
Stopping at the sad hotel that offers
No respite to despotic tyranny.

For many years you have silently swallowed
The bitter cassava of tyranny
Served to you at dagger-point.

Nightmare

Darkness chained me to my tattered reed mat;
The hand of tyranny sprinkled
The soot of ignorance in my eyes, and sleep
Hammered my head with slogans,
Then a nightmare stumbled on my sprawled life,
Tripped on the alarm of my heart,
And set me singing a healing song.

With song I bandage my ravaged land;
With the thread of song I sew the chopped heads
Back on the shoulders of the plucked flowers.
I plug the neck gash with a war chant;
With a sharp spear whose tongue sings,
I rip the veil of darkness from our land,
And the nightmare flees my secret light.

A Hanging
Zomba Central Prison

His pendulous body tolled
its own death knell from the rope
yet refused obstinately
to die, clinging desperately
to the last thread
of his condemned life.

That morning, oh!
his body sang until it could not
stand its own song;
like a guitar it hummed
and they could not but listen, stunned.
Every part of his body
opened its mouth and sang
death songs, Orphic heart songs,
shrill and sweet pent-up
songs of freedom, or sad and solemn
as the national anthem.

The heartstrings raised their harp
in a flood of insistent rhythm
and a slow drumming dance:
All his blood stood up and sang,
twisting towards the throat.
All the silent mouths raised their voices
and cried out their chorus.
No one could gag, or stop the prison
walls from singing;
No one could muzzle, or shield the ringing
echoes of Zomba mountain.
And the whispering pines on Queen's Point,
witnesses to the sordid deed,
raised their frosty mourning.

His heart was a cube of golden light,
a nest of incense where weaver-
birds had made their welcome permanent,
weaving a wall of thin silken tears
that sang with the lips of broken earth,
rolled waves, resistant and durable wind.

From every pore on his body a river of song,
or wail sprang and poured out.
His feet opened out like dark petals and chirped;
his fingers bloomed and plucked his heartstrings.
The song twined into the *makako* and jammed it
the looped noose would not close, numbed.

Being political, he was not entitled
to the miraculous luck of the criminals.
So they called in the prison doctor
to administer the *coup de grâce*.
He stabbed the chest with a thick
syringe and pumped the poison
into the heart with orgasmic release.

Stella Chipasula

I'm My Own Mother, Now

Mother, I am mothering you now;
Alone, I bear the burden of continuity.
Inside me, you are coiled
like a hard question without an answer.
On the far bank of the river
you sit silently, your mouth shut,
watching me struggle with this bundle
that grows like a giant seed, in me.
In your closed fist you hide
the riddles of the fruit or clay child
you told before you turned your back
and walked, fading, into the mist.
But, mother, I am mothering you now;
new generations pass through my blood,
and I bear you proudly on my back
where you are no longer a question.

Albert Kalimbakatha

Snail's Lament

Crumbled I die
Tortured I die
Out in the dark.

Crumbled I die
Tortured I die
Out in the rain.

Crumbled I die
Tortured I die
Away from green
Grassland home.

Crumbled I die
Tortured I die
On muddy roads

Crumbled I die
Tortured I die
In innocence.

Crumbled I die
Tortured I die
Under man's foot.

Mali

Ouologuem Yambo

When Negro Teeth Speak

Everyone thinks me a cannibal
But you know how people talk

Everyone sees my red gums but who
Has white ones
Up with tomatoes

Everyone says fewer tourists will come
Now
But you know
We aren't in America and anyway everyone
Is broke

Everyone says it's my fault and is afraid
But look
My teeth are white not red
I haven't eaten anyone

People are wicked and say I gobble
the tourists roasted
Or perhaps grilled
Roasted or grilled I asked them
They fell silent and looked fearfully at my gums
Up with tomatoes

Everyone knows an arable country has agriculture
Up with vegetables

Everyone maintains that vegetables
Don't nourish the grower well
And that I am well-grown for an undeveloped man
Miserable vermin living on tourists
Down with my teeth

Everyone suddenly surrounded me
Fettered
Thrown down prostrated
At the feet of justice

Cannibal or not cannibal
Speak up
Ah you think yourself clever
And try to look proud

Now we'll see you get what's coming to you
What is your last word
Poor condemned man

I shouted up with tomatoes

The men were cruel and the women curious you see
There was one in the peering circle
Who with her voice rattling like the lid of a casserole
Screamed
Yelped
Open him up
I'm sure papa is still inside

The knives being blunt
Which is understandable among vegetarians
Like the Westerners
They grabbed a Gillette blade
And patiently
Crisss
Crasss
Floccc
They opened my belly

A plantation of tomatoes was growing there
Irrigated by streams of palm wine
Up with tomatoes

Mauritania

Oumar Ba

Justice is Done

Beaten up,
Robbed,
Hospitalized?
And the witnesses?
Many as grains of the sand:
Kadiel is one;
Ndoulla
Ndyam Bele is one
Even the birds can testify . . .
But you forget that the chief
Has his son as the judge
And his son-in-law as interpreter.

Familiar Oxen

You tell me you have right on your side?
And those oxen that I see
In the chief's herd?
If I call them
They will respond to their baptismal names.

The Ox-Soldier

Don't you know
That an ox of seven seasons
Can become a soldier
And take your place for military service?

Nobility

One mustn't confuse the day and the night;
Nor even the fingers
Which are distinguished by their breadth and height.
Neither use of your language
Nor uniform
Bestows power, or birth, or character
On the son of a slave.
You have abolished slavery
Just to subjugate us
To the offspring of our captives.
Commander,
I am the son of my father
Who died in that prison.
France, they say, is justice.
But they see us without eyes,
Through the eyes of others
Billahi! seven times Billahi!
Drive from your service
Those tailless dogs!
Listen to those who do not love you
But whose word is invulnerable
As the centenarian caïlcedrat
Of Salde.
You will have the truth.

Mauritius

Edouard Maunick

Two poems from *Les Manèges de la mer* (1964)

6

Further off is the measured force the word of the sea
Further without leeway for the blueing shoulders of the horizon

harm is born of the light
when it capsizes under the voyages' assault
when it watches oblivion like a beast
and seeks the shipwreck of ten-year-old villages
conclusive shifts of time in exile

further off is risk without defeat
the ever renewed patience of the shadow
to find words beyond language
further the serpent in the blood
broken by all the betrayals
victories of voluntary resignation

I did not leave in order to forget
I am mulatto
the Indian ocean will never give way to the city of today
but harm compromises in me harm however come by

I repeat further off to stain the liquid mirrors
to cross a threshold where you await me since the poem

20

I love to encounter you in strange cities
where every broil every noise every clock
betrays your body beating in my pulses
I love to release you in foreign beds
when night becomes a tree by the force of its nudity

I love what separates us in our resemblance
frontiers of dawn resembling our faces
the proofs of life are only found elsewhere
never say no when I speak to you from afar . . .

Mozambique

José Craveirinha

The Seed is in Me

Dead or living
the seed is in me
in the universal whiteness of my bones

All feel
uneasiness
at the undoubted whiteness of my bones
white as the breasts of Ingrids or Marias
in Scandinavian lands
or in Polana the smart quarter
of my old native town.

All feel
uneasiness
that the mingling in my veins should be
blood from the blood of every blood
and instead of the peace ineffable of pure and simple birth
and a pure and simple death
breed a rash of complexes
from the seed of my bones.

But a night with the massaleiras heavy with green fruit
batuques swirl above the sweating stones
and the tears of rivers

All feel
uneasiness
at the white seed in me
breeding a rash inflamed with malediction.

And one day
will come all the Marias of the distant nations
penitent or no
weeping
laughing
or loving to the rhythm of a song

To say to my bones
forgive us, brother.

Three Dimensions

In the cabin . . .
the god of the machine
in cap and overalls
holds in his hand the secret of the pistons.

In the carriage . . .
the first-class god
elaborates his schemes in regulated air.

And on the branch-line . . .
– feet flat against the steel of the coaches –
bursting his lungs
the god of the trolley.

Noémia de Sousa

Appeal

Who has strangled the tired voice
of my forest sister?
On a sudden, her call to action
was lost in the endless flow of night and day.
No more it reaches me every morning,
wearied with long journeying,
mile after mile drowned
in the everlasting cry: Macala!

No, it comes no more, still damp with dew,
leashed with children and submission . . .
One child on her back, another in her womb
– always, always, always!
And a face all compassed in a gentle look,
whenever I recall that look I feel
my flesh and blood swell tremulous,
throbbing to revelations and affinities . . .
– But who has stopped her immeasurable look
from feeding my deep hunger after comradeship
that my poor table never will serve to satisfy?

Io mamane, who can have shot the noble voice
of my forest sister?
What mean and brutal rhino-whip
has lashed until it killed her?

– In my garden the seringa blooms.
But with an evil omen in its purple flower,
in its intense inhuman scent;
and the wrap of tenderness spread by the sun

over the light mat of petals
has waited since summer for my sister's child
to rest himself upon it . . .
In vain, in vain,
a chirico sings and sings perched among the garden reeds,
for the little boy of my missing sister,
the victim of the forest's vaporous dawns.
Ah, I know, I know: at the last there was a litter
of farewell in those gentle eyes,
and her voice came like a murmur hoarse,
tragic and despairing . . .

O Africa, my motherland, answer me:
What was done to my forest sister,
that she comes no more to the city with her eternal little ones
(one on her back, one in her womb),
with her eternal charcoal-vendor's cry?
O Africa, my motherland,
you at least will not forsake my heroic sister,
she shall live in the proud memorial of your arms!

If You Want to Know Me

If you want to know who I am,
examine with careful eyes
that piece of black wood
which an unknown Maconde brother
with inspired hands
carved and worked
in distant lands to the North.

Ah, she is who I am:
empty eye sockets despairing of possessing life
a mouth slashed with wounds of anguish,
enormous, flattened hands,
raised as though to implore and threaten,

body tattooed with visible and invisible scars
by the hard whips of slavery . . .
tortured and magnificent,
proud and mystical,
Africa from head to toe,
— ah, she is who I am!

If you want to understand me
come and bend over my African soul,
in the groans of the Negroes on the docks
in the frenzied dances of the Chopes
in the rebelliousness of the Shanganas
in the strange melancholy evaporating
from a native song, into the night . . .

And ask me nothing more
if you really wish to know me . . .
for I am no more than a shell of flesh
in which the revolt of Africa congealed
its cry swollen with hope

Valente Ngwenya Malangatana

To the Anxious Mother

Into your arms I came
when you bore me, very anxious
you, who were so alarmed
at that monstrous moment
fearing that God might take me.
Everyone watched in silence
to see if the birth was going well
everyone washed their hands
to be able to receive the one who came from Heaven
and all the women were still and afraid.
But when I emerged
from the place where you sheltered me so long
at once I drew my first breath
at once you cried out with joy
the first kiss was my grandmother's.
And she took me at once to the place
where they kept me, hidden away
everyone was forbidden to enter my room
because everyone smelt bad
and I all fresh, fresh
breathed gently, wrapped in my napkins.
But grandmother, who seemed like a madwoman,
always looking and looking again
because the flies came at me
and the mosquitoes harried me
God who also watched over me
was my old granny's friend.

Woman

In the cool waters of the river
we shall have fish that are huge
which shall give the sign of
the end of the world perhaps
because they will make an end of woman
woman who adorns the fields
woman who is the fruit of man.

The flying fish makes an end of searching
because woman is the gold of man
when she sings she ever seems
like the fado-singer's well-tuned guitar
when she dies, I shall cut off
her hair to deliver me from sin.

Woman's hair shall be the blanket
over my coffin when another Artist
calls me to Heaven to paint me
woman's breasts shall be my pillow
woman's eye shall open up for me the way to heaven
woman's belly shall give birth to me up there
and woman's glance shall watch me
as I go up to Heaven.

Jorge Rebelo

Poem

Come, brother, and tell me your life
come, show me the marks of revolt
   which the enemy left on your body

Come, say to me 'Here
my hands have been crushed
because they defended
the land which they own'

'Here my body was tortured
because it refused to bend
to invaders'

'Here my mouth was wounded
because it dared to sing
my people's freedom'

Come, brother, and tell me your life,
come relate me the dreams of revolt
which you and your fathers and forefathers
dreamed
in silence
through shadowless nights made for love

Come tell me these dreams become
war,
the birth of heroes,
land reconquered,
mothers who, fearless,
send their sons to fight.

Come, tell me all this, my brother.

And later I will forge simple words
which even the children can understand
words which will enter every house
like the wind
and fall like red hot embers
on our people's souls.

In our land
Bullets are beginning to flower.

Poem for a Militant

Mother.
I have an iron rifle
your son,
the one you saw chained
one day
(When you cried as if
the chains bound and battered
your hands and feet)
Your boy is free now
Mother.
Your boy has an iron rifle,
My rifle
will break the chains
will open the prisons
will kill the tyrants
will win back our land
Mother,
Beauty is to fight for freedom,
Justice rings in my every shot
and ancient dreams awaken like birds.
Fighting, on the front,
Your image descends.
I fight for you,

Mother
to dry the tears
of your eyes.

Namibia

Mvula ya Nangolo

Robben Island

Dedicated to Comrade Andimba Toivo ya Toivo who spent eighteen years
of a twenty-year sentence on Robben Island.

Just how far is Robben Island from a black child at play?
What forces take his father there with all the world between?
Oh! Mother caution your warrior son again
or else he'll show his might

Just how far is Robben Island from the United Nations
    headquarters?
Have I time to ponder now when patriots are drilling fast?
Spears are flying and the shields are once more bloody
for the drums of war are beating again

Just how far is Robben Island from the London Stock Exchange?
You couldn't hear my talking war drums
for uselessly loud is the enemy's cannon roar

Just how far is Robben Island from the Yankee's White House?
I have no sight for I do not speak languages so foreign
the stars and zebra stripes are dazzling me
the US President speaks – his foreign secretary cheats

Then just how far is Robben Island from the field of Waterloo?
A few bushes away
a village or two in between
and the warrior son will take you there.

Guerrilla Promise

I'll rush upon you
like escaping newborn sunray
then dazzle you with my lethal swiftness
'cause I'm the Fight

As unknown as an unborn battle
labouring with steel and hand grenade
I'm death conceived

'til my moment arrives
with pain . . . blood and terror
I'm a soldier of this realm
I'm a poisoned arrow

I'm a string-bow
I'm a sharpened spear
I'm a sword
waiting in my sheath
only for your death.

Nigeria

Gabriel Okara

The Snowflakes Sail Gently Down

The snowflakes sail gently
down from the misty eye of the sky
and fall lightly lightly on the
winter-weary elms. And the branches
winter-stripped and nude, slowly
with the weight of the weightless snow
bow like grief-stricken mourners
as white funeral cloth is slowly
unrolled over deathless earth.
And dead sleep stealthily from the
heater rose and closed my eyes with
the touch of silk cotton on water falling.

Then I dreamed a dream
in my dead sleep. But I dreamed
not of earth dying and elms a vigil
keeping. I dreamed of birds, black
birds flying in my inside, nesting
and hatching on oil palms bearing suns
for fruits and with roots denting the
uprooters' spades. And I dreamed the
uprooters tired and limp, leaning on my roots –
their abandoned roots
and the oil palms gave them each a sun.

But on their palms
they balanced the blinding orbs
and frowned with schisms on their
brows – for the suns reached not
the brightness of gold!

Then I awoke. I awoke
to the silently falling snow
and bent-backed elms bowing and
swaying to the winter wind like
white-robed Moslems salaaming at evening
prayer, and the earth lying inscrutable
like the face of a god in a shrine.

Adhiambo

I hear many voices
like it's said a madman hears;
I hear trees talking
like it's said a medicine man hears.

Maybe I'm a madman,
I'm a medicine man.

Maybe I'm mad,
for the voices are luring me,
urging me from the midnight
moon and the silence of my desk
to walk on wave crests across a sea.

Maybe I'm a medicine man
hearing talking saps,
seeing behind trees;
but who's lost his powers
of invocation.

But the voices and the trees
are now name-spelling and one figure
silence-etched across
the moonface is walking, stepping
over continents and seas.

And I raised my hand –
my trembling hand, gripping
my heart as handkerchief
and waved and waved – and waved –
but she turned her eyes away.

Spirit of the Wind

The storks are coming now –
white specks in the silent sky.
They had gone north seeking
fairer climes to build their homes
when here was raining.

They are back with me now –
Spirits of the wind,
beyond the gods' confining
hands they go north and west and east,
instinct guiding.

But willed by the gods
I'm sitting on this rock
watching them come and go
from sunrise to sundown, with the spirit
urging within.

And urging a red pool stirs,
and each ripple is
the instinct's vital call,
a desire in a million cells
confined.

O God of the gods and me,
shall I not heed
this prayer-bell call, the noon
angelus, because my stork is caged
in Singed Hair and Dark Skin?

One Night at Victoria Beach

The wind comes rushing from the sea,
the waves curling like mambas strike
the sands and recoiling hiss in rage
washing the Aladuras'* feet pressing hard
on the sand and with eyes fixed hard
on what only hearts can see, they shouting
pray, the Aladuras pray; and coming
from booths behind, compelling highlife
forces ears; and car lights startle pairs
arm in arm passing washer-words back
and forth like haggling sellers and buyers –

Still they pray, the Aladuras pray
with hands pressed against their hearts
and their white robes pressed against
their bodies by the wind; and drinking
palm-wine and beer, the people boast
at bars at the beach. Still they pray.
They pray, the Aladuras pray
to what only hearts can see while dead
fishermen long dead with bones rolling
nibbled clean by nibbling fishes, follow
four dead cowries shining like stars
into deep sea where fishes sit in judgement;
and living fishermen in dark huts
sit round dim lights with Babalawo
throwing their souls in four cowries
on sand, trying to see tomorrow.

Still, they pray, the Aladuras pray
to what only hearts can see behind
the curling waves and the sea, the stars
and the subduing unanimity of the sky
and their white bones beneath the sand.

* Aladuras: a Christian sect addicted to ritual bathing.

And standing dead on dead sands,
I felt my knees touch living sands –
but the rushing wind killed the budding words.

Moon in the Bucket

Look!
Look out there
in the bucket
the rusty bucket
with water unclean

Look!
A luminous plate is floating –
the Moon, dancing to the gentle night wind
Look! all you who shout across the wall
with a million hates. Look at the dancing moon
It is peace unsoiled by the murk
and dirt of this bucket war.

Christopher Okigbo

Six poems from *Heavensgate* (1961)

Overture

Before you, mother Idoto,
naked I stand,
before your watery presence,
a prodigal,

leaning on an oilbean,
lost in your legend . . .

Under your power wait I
     on barefoot,
watchman for the watchword
     at heavensgate;

out of the depths my cry
give ear and hearken.

Eyes Watch the Stars

Eyes open on the beach,
eyes open, of the prodigal;
upward to heaven shoot
where stars will fall from.

Which secret I have told into no ear;
    into a dughole to hold,
     not to drown with –
Which secret I have planted into beachsand;

> now breaks
salt-white surf on the stones and me,
>> and lobsters and shells in
>> iodine smell –
>> maid of the salt-emptiness,
>> sophisticreamy, native,

whose secret I have covered up with beachsand.

> Shadow of rain
> over sunbeaten beach,
> shadow of rain
> over man with woman.

Water Maid

Bright
with the armpit dazzle of a lioness,
she answers,
wearing white light about her;
and the waves escort her,
my lioness,
crowned with moonlight.

So brief her presence –
match-flare in wind's breath –
so brief with mirrors around me.

Downward . . .
the waves distil her:
gold crop
sinking ungathered.

Watermaid of the salt emptiness,
grown are the ears of the secret.

Sacrifice

Thundering drums and cannons
in palm grove:
the spirit is in ascent.

I have visited,
on palm beam imprinted
my pentagon –

I have visited, the prodigal . . .

In palm grove
long drums and cannons:
the spirit in the ascent.

Lustra

So would I to the hills again
so would I
to where springs the fountain
there to draw from
and to hilltop clamber
body and soul
whitewashed in the moondew
there to see from

So would I from my eye the mist
so would I
through moonmist to hilltop
there for the cleansing

Here is a new-laid egg
here a white hen at midterm.

Bridge

I am standing above you and tide
    above the noontide,
Listening to the laughter of waters
    that do not know why:

Listening to incense . . .

I am standing above the noontide
    with my head above it,
Under my feet float the waters:
    tide blows them under.

Four poems from _Limits_ (1962)

Siren Limits

I

Suddenly becoming talkative
    like weaverbird
Summoned at offside of
        dream remembered

Between sleep and waking,
I hang up my egg-shells
To you of palm grove,

Upon whose bamboo towers
Hang, dripping with yesterupwine

A tiger mask and nude spear . . .

Queen of the damp half-light,
    I have had my cleansing,
Emigrant with airborne nose,
    The he-goat-on-heat.

2

For he was a shrub among the poplars,
Needing more roots
More sap to grow to sunlight,
Thirsting for sunlight

A low growth among the forest.

Into the soul
The selves extended their branches
Into the moments of each living hour
Feeling for audience

Straining thin among the echoes;

And out of the solitude
Voice and soul with selves unite,
Riding the echoes,

Horsemen of the apocalypse,

And crowned with one self
The name displays its foliage,
Hanging low

A green cloud above the forest.

3

Banks of reed.
Mountains of broken bottles.

    & the mortar is not yet dry . . .

Silent the footfall
soft as cat's paw,
Sandalled in velvet,
    in fur

So we must go,
Wearing evemist against the shoulders,
Trailing sun's dust sawdust of combat,
With brand burning out at hand-end.

 & the mortar is not yet dry . . .

Then we must sing
Tongue-tied without name or audience,
Making harmony among the branches.

And this is the crisis-point,
The twilight moment between
   sleep and waking;
And voice that is reborn transpires
Not thro' pores in the flesh
   but the soul's backbone

Hurry on down
   through the high-arched gate –
Hurry on down
   little stream to the lake;
Hurry on down –
   through the cinder market
Hurry on down
   in the wake of the dream;
Hurry on down –
   To rockpoint of CABLE
   To pull by the rope
   The big white elephant . . .

 & the mortar is not yet dry
 & the mortar is not yet dry . . .

& the dream wakes
 & the voice fades
In the damp half-light,
 Like a shadow,

Not leaving a mark.

4

An image insists
    from the flag-pole of the heart,
The image distracts
    with the cruelty of the rose ...

    My lioness,
(No shield is lead-plate against you)
Wound me with your seaweed face
    Blinded like a strongroom.

Distances of your
    arm-pit fragrance
Turn chloroform,
    enough for my patience –

When you have finished,
& done up my stitches
Wake me near the altar
    & this poem will be finished.

From Lament of the Drums (1964)

I

Lion-hearted cedar forest, gonads for our thunder,
Even if you are very far away, we invoke you:

Give us our hollow heads of long-drums ...

Antelopes for the cedar forest, swifter messengers
Than flash-of-beacon-flame, we invoke you:

Hide us; deliver us from our nakedness ...

Many-fingered canebrake, exile for our laughter,
Even if you are very far away, we invoke you:

Come; limber our raw hides of antelopes ...

Thunder of tanks of giant iron steps of detonators,
Fail safe from the clearing, we implore you:

We are tuned for a feast-of-seven-souls . . .

Two poems from *Distances* (1964)

1

From flesh into phantom,
on the horizontal stone:

I was the sole witness to my homecoming . . .

Serene lights on the other balcony –
redolent fountains, bristling with signs.
But what does my divine rejoicing hold?
A bowl of incense? A nest of fireflies?

I was the sole witness to my homecoming . . .

And in the inflorescence of the white chamber,
a voice, from very far away, chanted, and the chamber descanted
the birthday of earth, paddling me home through
some dark labyrinth, from laughter to the dream.

Miner into my solitude, incarnate
voice of the dream, you will go,
with me as your chief acolyte,
again into the ant-hole . . .

I was the sole witness to my homecoming . . .

2

Death lay in ambush,
that evening in that island;
and the voice sought its echo,
that evening in that island,
and the eye lost its light,
and the light lost its shadow.

And the wind, eternal suitor of dead leaves,
unrolled his bandages to the finest swimmer . . .

And it was an evening without flesh or skeleton;
an evening with no silver bells to its tale;
without lanterns; without buntings;
and it was an evening without age or memory –

for we are talking of such commonplace things,
and on the brink of such great events –
and in the freezing tuberoses of the white
chamber, eyes that had lost their animal
colour – havoc of incandescent rays –
pinned me, cold to the marble stretcher,
     until my eyes lost their blood,
      and the blood lost its odour;
and the everlasting fire from the oblong window
forgot the taste of ash in the air's marrow . . .

Anguish and solitude . . .
Smothered, my scattered
cry, the dancers,
lost among their own
snares; the faces,
the hands, held captive;
the interspaces
reddening with blood . . .

And behind them all,
in smock of white cotton,
Death herself,
the chief celebrant,
in a cloud of incense,
paring her fingernails . . .

At her feet roll their heads like cut fruits;
about her fall
their severed members, numerous as locusts.

Like split wood left to dry,
the dismembered joints
of the ministrants pile high.

She bathes her knees in the blood of attendants,
her smock in the entrails of the ministrants . . .

Two poems from *Path of Thunder* (1967)

Come Thunder

Now that the triumphant march has entered the last street corners,
Remember, O dancers, the thunder among the clouds . . .

Now that the laughter, broken in two, hangs tremulous between
  the teeth,
Remember, O dancers, the lightning beyond the earth . . .

The smell of blood already floats in the lavender-mist of the
  afternoon.
The death sentence lies in ambush along the corridors of power;
And a great fearful thing already tugs at the cables of the open air,
A nebula immense and immeasurable, a night of deep waters –
An iron dream unnamed and unprintable, a path of stone.

The drowsy heads of the pods in barren farmlands witness it,
The homesteads abandoned in this century's brush fire witness it:
The myriad eyes of deserted corn cobs in burning barns witness it:
Magic birds with the miracle of lightning flash on their feathers . . .

The arrows of God tremble at the gates of light,
The drums of curfew pander to a dance of death;

And the secret thing in its heaving
Threatens with iron mask
The last lighted torch of the century . . .

Elegy for Alto
With drum accompaniment

AND THE HORN may now paw the air howling goodbye . . .

For the Eagles are now in sight:
Shadows in the horizon –

THE ROBBERS are here in black sudden steps of showers, of
    caterpillars –

THE EAGLES have come again,
The eagles rain down on us –

POLITICIANS are back in giant hidden steps of howitzers, of
    detonators –

THE EAGLES descend on us,
Bayonets and cannons –

THE ROBBERS descend on us to strip us of our laughter, of our
    thunder –

THE EAGLES have chosen their game,
Taken our concubines –

POLITICIANS are here in this iron dance of mortars, of
    generators –

THE EAGLES are suddenly there,
New stars of iron dawn;

So let the horn paw the air howling goodbye . . .

O mother mother Earth, unbind me; let this be
    my last testament; let this be
The ram's hidden wish to the sword the sword's
    secret prayer to the scabbard –

THE ROBBERS are back in black hidden steps of detonators –

FOR BEYOND the blare of sirened afternoons, beyond
    the motorcades;
Beyond the voices and days, the echoing highways; beyond the
    latescence
Of our dissonant airs; through our curtained eyeballs,
    through our shuttered sleep,
On to our forgotten selves, on to our broken images;
    beyond the barricades
Commandments and edicts, beyond the iron tables,
    beyond the elephant's
Legendary patience, beyond his inviolable bronze
    bust; beyond our crumbling towers –

BEYOND the iron path careering along the same beaten track –

THE GLIMPSE of a dream lies smouldering in a cave,
    together with the mortally wounded birds.
Earth, unbind me; let me be the prodigal; let this be
    the ram's ultimate prayer to the tether . . .

AN OLD STAR departs, leaves us here on the shore
Gazing heavenward for a new star approaching;
The new star appears, foreshadows its going
Before a going and coming that goes on for ever . . .

Wole Soyinka

Death in the Dawn

Traveller, you must set out
At dawn. And wipe your feet upon
The dog-nose wetness of the earth.

Let sunrise quench your lamps. And watch
Faint brush pricklings in the sky light
Cottoned feet to break the early earthworm
On the hoe. Now shadows stretch with sap
Not twilight's death and sad prostration.
This soft kindling, soft receding breeds
Racing joys and apprehensions for
A naked day. Burdened hulks retract,
Stoop to the mist in faceless throng
To wake the silent markets – swift, mute
Processions on grey byways . . . On this
Counterpane, it was –
Sudden winter at the death
Of dawn's lone trumpeter. Cascades
Of white feather-flakes . . . but it proved
A futile rite. Propitiation sped
Grimly on, before.
The right foot for joy, the left, dread
And the mother prayed, Child
May you never walk
When the road waits, famished.

Traveller, you must set forth
At dawn.
I promise marvels of the holy hour
Presages as the white cock's flapped
Perverse impalement – as who would dare
The wrathful wings of man's Progression . . .

But such another wraith! Brother,
Silenced in the startled hug of
Your invention – is this mocked grimace
This closed contortion – I?

Massacre, October '66

Written in Tegel

Shards of sunlight touch me here
Shredded in willows. Through stained-glass
Fragments on the lake I sought to reach
A mind at silt-bed

The lake stayed cold
I swam in an October flush of dying leaves
The gardener's labour flew in seasoned scrolls
Lettering the wind

Swept from painted craft
A mockery of waves remarked this idyll sham
I trod on acorns; each shell's detonation
Aped the skull's uniqueness.

Came sharper reckoning –
This favoured food of hogs cannot number high
As heads still harshly crop to whirlwinds
I have briefly fled

The oak rains a hundred more
A kind confusion to arithmetics of death:
Time to watch autumn the removal man
Dust down rare canvases

To let a loud resolve of passion
Fly to a squirrel, burnished light and copper fur
A distant stance without the lake's churchwindows
And for a stranger, love.

A host of acorns fell, silent
As they are silenced all, whose laughter
Rose from such indifferent paths, oh God
They are not strangers all

Whose desecration mocks the word
Of peace – *salaam aleikun* – not strangers any
Brain of thousands pressed asleep to pig fodder –
Shun pork the unholy – cries the priest.

I borrow seasons of an alien land
In brotherhood of ill, pride of race around me
Strewn in sunlit shards. I borrow alien lands
To stay the season of a mind.

Civilian and Soldier

My apparition rose from the fall of lead,
Declared, 'I'm a civilian.' It only served
To aggravate your fright. For how could I
Have risen, a being of this world, in that hour
Of impartial death! And I thought also: nor is
Your quarrel of this world.

                                        You stood still
For both eternities, and oh I heard the lesson
Of your training sessions, cautioning –
Scorch earth behind you, do not leave
A dubious neutral to the rear. Reiteration
Of my civilian quandary, burrowing earth
From the lead festival of your more eager friends
Worked the worse on your confusion, and when
You brought the gun to bear on me, and death

Twitched me gently in the eye, your plight
And all of you came clear to me.

                              I hope some day
Intent upon my trade of living, to be checked
In stride by *your* apparition in a trench,
Signalling, I am a soldier. No hesitation then
But I shall shoot you clean and fair
With meat and bread, a gourd of wine
A bunch of breasts from either arm, and that
Lone question – do you friend, even now, know
What it is all about?

Prisoner

Grey, to the low grass cropping
Slung, wet-lichened, wisps from such
Smoke heaviness, elusive of thin blades
Curl inward to the earth, breed
The grey hours,
And days, and years, for do not
The wise grey temples we must build
To febrile years, here begin, not
In tears and ashes, but on the sad mocking
Threads, compulsive of the hour?

In the desert wildness, when, lone cactus,
Cannibal was his love – even amidst the
Crag and gorge, the leap and night-tremors
Even as the potsherd stayed and the sandstorm
Fell – intimations came.

In the whorled centre of the storm, a threnody
But not from this. For that far companion,
Made sudden stranger when the wind slacked
And the centre fell, grief. And the stricken
Potsherd lay, disconsolate – intimations then

But not from these. He knew only
Sudden seizure. And time conquest
Bound him helpless to each grey essence.

Nothing remained if pains and longings
Once, once set the walls. Sadness
Closed him, rootless, lacking cause.

Season

Rust is ripeness, rust
And the wilted corn-plume;
Pollen is mating-time when swallows
Weave a dance
Of feathered arrows
Thread corn-stalks in winged
Streaks of light. And, we loved to hear
Spliced phrases of the wind, to hear
Rasps in the field, where corn leaves
Pierce like bamboo slivers.

Now, garnerers we,
Awaiting rust on tassels, draw
Long shadows from the dusk, wreathe
Dry thatch in woodsmoke. Laden stalks
Ride the germ's decay – we await
The promise of the rust.

Night

Your hand is heavy, Night, upon my brow,
I bear no heart mercuric like the clouds, to dare
Exacerbation from your subtle plough.

Woman as a clam, on the sea's crescent
I saw your jealous eye quench the sea's
Fluorescence, dance on the pulse incessant

Of the waves. And I stood, drained
Submitting like the sands, blood and brine
Coursing to the roots. Night, you rained

Serrated shadows through dank leaves
Till, bathed in warm suffusion of your dappled cells
Sensations pained me, faceless, silent as night thieves.

Hide me now, when night children haunt the earth
I must hear none! These misted calls will yet
Undo me; naked, unbidden, at Night's muted birth.

Abiku*

In vain your bangles cast
Charmed circles at my feet
I am Abiku, calling for the first
And the repeated time.

Must I weep for goats and cowries
For palm oil and the sprinkled ash?
Yams do not sprout in amulets
To earth Abiku's limbs.

So when the snail is burnt in his shell,
Whet the heated fragment, brand me
Deeply on the breast. You must know him
When Abiku calls again.

* Abiku: a 'spirit child'; one fated to a cycle of early death and rebirth to the same mother.

I am the squirrel teeth, cracked
The riddle of the palm. Remember
This, and dig me deeper still into
The god's swollen foot.

Once and the repeated time, ageless
Though I puke; and when you pour
Libations, each finger points me near
The way I came, where

The ground is wet with mourning
White dew suckles flesh-birds
Evening befriends the spider, trapping
Flies in wind-froth;

Night, and Abiku sucks the oil
From lamps. Mothers! I'll be the
Suppliant snake coiled on the doorstep
Yours the killing cry.

The ripest fruit was saddest;
Where I crept, the warmth was cloying.
In the silence of webs, Abiku moans, shaping
Mounds from the yolk.

Four poems from *A Shuttle in the Crypt* (1972)

Ujamaa
(for Julius Nyerere)

Sweat is leaven for the earth
Not tribute. Earth replete
Seeks no homage from the toil of earth.
Sweat is leaven for the earth
Not driven homage to a fortressed god.

Your black earth hands unchain
Hope from death messengers, from
In-bred dogmanoids that prove
Grimmer than the Grim Reaper, insatiate
Predators on humanity, their fodder.
Sweat is leaven, bread, Ujamaa
Bread of the earth, by the earth
For the earth. Earth is all people.

Bearings III: Amber Wall

Breath of the sun, crowned
In green crepes and amber beads
Children's voices at the door of Orient

Raising eyelids on the sluggish earth
Dispersing sulphur fumes above the lake
Of awakening, you come hunting with the sun

His hands upon the loftiest branches
Halted on the prize, eyes in wonderlust
Questioned this mystery of man's isolation

Fantasies richer than burning mangoes
Flickered through his royal mind, an open
Noon above the door that closed

I would you may discover, mid-morning
To the man's estate, with lesser pain
The wall of gain within the outer loss

Your flutes at evening, your seed-awakening
Dances fill the night with growth; I hear
The sun's sad chorus to your starlit songs

Hanging Day: Procession

I

Hanging day. A hollow earth
Echoes footsteps of the grave procession
Walls in sunspots
Lean to shadows of the shortening morn

Behind, an eyepatch lushly blue.
The wall of prayer has taken refuge
In a peace of blindness, closed
Its grey recessive deeps. Fretful limbs

And glances that would sometimes
Conjure up a drawbridge
Raised but never lowered between
Their gathering and my sway

Withdraw, as all the living world
Belie their absence in a feel of eyes
Barred and secret in the empty home
Of shuttered windows. I know the heart
Has journeyed far from present

Tread. Drop. Dread Drop. Dead

What may I tell you? What reveal?
I who before them peered unseen
Who stood one-legged on the untrodden
Verge – lest I should not return.

That I received them? That I
Wheeled above and flew beneath them
And brought them on their way
And came to mine, even to the edge
Of the unspeakable encirclement?
What may I tell you of the five
Bell-ringers on the ropes to chimes
Of silence?

What tell you of rigours of the law?
From watchtowers on stunted walls,
Raised to stay a siege of darkness
What whisper to their football thunders
Vanishing to shrouds of sunlight?

    Let no man speak of justice, guilt.
    Far away, blood-stained in their
    Tens of thousands, hands that damned
    These wretches to the pit triumph
    But here, alone the solitary deed.

I Anoint My Flesh
(Tenth Day of Fast)

I anoint my flesh
Thought is hallowed in the lean
Oil of solitude
I call you forth, all, upon
Terraces of light. Let the dark
Withdraw

I anoint my voice
And let it sound hereafter
Or dissolve upon its lonely passage
In your void. Voices new
Shall rouse the echoes when
Evil shall again arise

I anoint my heart
Within its flame I lay
Spent ashes of your hate –
Let evil die.

John Pepper Clark

Eight poems from *A Reed in the Tide* (1965)

Ibadan

Ibadan,
      running splash of rust
and gold – flung and scattered
among seven hills like broken
china in the sun.

*Olokun**

I love to pass my fingers,
As tide through weeds of the sea
And wind the tall fern-fronds
Through the strands of your hair
Dark as night that screens the naked moon:

I am jealous and passionate
Like Jehovah, God of the Jews,
And I would that you realize
No greater love had woman
From man than the one I have for you!

But what wakeful eyes of man,
Made of the mud of this earth,

---

* Olokun: goddess of the sea.

Can stare at the touch of sleep
The sable vehicle of dream
Which indeed is the look of your eyes?

So drunken, like ancient walls
We crumble in heaps at your feet;
And as the good maid of the sea,
Full of rich bounties for men,
You lift us all beggars to your breast.

Night Rain

What time of night it is
I do not know
Except that like some fish
Doped out of the deep
I have bobbed up bellywise
From stream of sleep
And no cocks crow.
It is drumming hard here
And I suppose everywhere
Droning with insistent ardour upon
Our roof-thatch and shed
And through sheaves slit open
To lightning and rafters
I cannot make out overhead
Great water drops are dribbling
Falling like orange or mango
Fruits showered forth in the wind
Or perhaps I should say so
Much like beads I could in prayer tell
Them on string as they break
In wooden bowls and earthenware
Mother is busy now deploying
About our roomlet and floor.

Although it is so dark
I know her practised step as
She moves her bins, bags, and vats
Out of the run of water
That like ants filing out of the wood
Will scatter and gain possession
Of the floor. Do not tremble then
But turn brothers, turn upon your side
Of the loosening mats
To where the others lie.
We have drunk tonight of a spell
Deeper than the owl's or bat's
That wet of wings may not fly.
Bedraggled upon the *iroko*, they stand
Emptied of hearts, and
Therefore will not stir, no, not
Even at dawn for then
They must scurry in to hide.
So we'll roll over on our back
And again roll to the beat
Of drumming all over the land
And under its ample soothing hand
Joined to that of the sea
We will settle to sleep of the innocent and free.

For Granny (from Hospital)

Tell me, before the ferryman's return,
What was that stirred within your soul,
One night fifteen floods today,
When upon a dugout
Mid pilgrim lettuce on the Niger,
You with a start strained me to breast:
Did you that night in the raucous voice
Of yesterday's rain,

Tumbling down banks of reed
To feed a needless stream,
Then recognize the loud note of quarrels
And endless dark nights of intrigue
In Father's house of many wives?
Or was it wonder at those footless stars
Who in their long translucent fall
Make shallow silten floors
Beyond the pale of muddy waters
Appear more plumbless than the skies?

Cry of Birth

An echo of childhood stalks before me
like evening shadows on the earth,
rolling back into piquant memory
the anguished cry of my birth;

Out of the caverns of nativity
a voice, I little knew as my own
and thought to have shed with infancy,
returns with a sharpness before unknown.

Poor castaways to this darkling shore,
void out of the sea of eternity
and blind, we catch by reflex horror
an instant glimpse, the guilt of our see:

The souls of men are steeped in stupor
who, tenants upon this wild isle unblest,
sleep on, oblivious of its loud nightmare
with wanton motions bedevilling our breast.

All night, through its long reaches and black
I wander as Io, driven by strange passions,
within and out, and for gadfly have at my back
one harrowing shriek of pain and factions –

It comes ceaseless as from the wilderness!
commingled with the vague cogitation
of the sea, its echo of despair and stress
precedes me like a shade to the horizon.

Abiku

Coming and going these several seasons,
Do stay out on the baobab tree,
Follow where you please your kindred spirits
If indoors it is not enough for you.
True, it leaks through the thatch
When floods brim the banks,
And the bats and the owls
Often tear in at night through the eaves,
And at harmattan, the bamboo walls
Are ready tinder for the fire
That dries the fresh fish up on the rack.
Still, it's been the healthy stock
To several fingers, to many more will be
Who reach to the sun.
No longer then bestride the threshold
But step in and stay
For good. We know the knife-scars
Serrating down your back and front
Like beak of the sword-fish,
And both your ears, notched
As a bondsman to this house,
Are all relics of your first comings.
Then step in, step in and stay
For her body is tired,
Tired, her milk going sour
Where many more mouths gladden the heart.

A Child Asleep

He who plucked light
From under shade of a tree
Sat so in dust, but in silence,
Passing like a spear clean into
The pith of things. But you,
Graft to an old bombax tree,
Raised on fulness of sap science
Cannot give, breed flies
In the oil of our evening,
Have sat dropsical feeding
On desire: it squashes, like dried
Out ribs of tobacco an old woman
Is turning into snuff you tried
To wreck with stones –
But oh look at what we spies
Have missed! In the sand
Here at our feet already fallen is
Your stool, and how clean
Past our fingers, teasing and
Tugging, you have slumped down
A natal stump, there shed
Distended in the dust – No!
As a primeval shadow
Tumbling head over heels into arms of light.

The Leader

They have felled him to the ground
Who announced home from abroad
Wrestled to a standstill his champion
Cousin the Killer of Cows. Yes,
In all that common
And swamp, pitched piecemeal by storks,

No iguana during a decade of tongues
Could throw or twist him round
While he rallied the race and clan.
Now like an alligator he lies
Trussed up in a house without eyes
And ears:
        Bit of bamboo,
Flung to laggard dogs by drowning
Nearest of kin, has quite locked his jaws.

From *Casualties* (1970)

Season of Omens

When calabashes held petrol and men
   turned faggots in the streets
Then came the five hunters
When mansions and limousines made
   bonfires in sunset cities
Then came the five hunters
When clans were discovered that were not in the book
   and cattle counted for heads of men
Then came the five hunters
When hoodlums took possession of police barracks
   in defiance of bullets
Then came the five hunters
When ministers legislated from bed and
   made high office the prize for failure
Then came the five hunters
When wads of notes were kept in infant skulls
   with full blessing of prelates
Then came the five hunters
When women grew heavy with ballot papers delivering
   the house entire to adulterers
Then came the five hunters

When a grand vizier in season of arson turned
   upon bandits in a far off place
Then came the five hunters
When men lost their teeth before they cut them
   to eat corn
Then came the five hunters
When a cabinet grew so broad the top gave way
   and trapped everyone therein
Then came the five hunters

At club closure,
Antelopes slept, for lions snored;
Then struck the five hunters,
But not together, not together.
One set out on his own into the night,
Four down their different spoors by the sea;
By light of stars at dawn
Each read in the plan a variant

And so one morning
The people woke up to a great smoke.
There was fire all right,
But who lighted it, where
The lighter of the fire?

Fallen in the grass was the lion,
Fallen in the forest was the jackal,
Missing by the sea was the shepherd-sheep,
His castrate ram in tow,
And all around was the blood of hounds.

Frank Aig-Imoukhuede

One Wife for One Man

I done try go church, I done go for court
Dem all day talk about di 'new culture':
Dem talk about 'equality', dem mention 'divorce'
Dem holler am so-tay my ear nearly cut;
    One wife be for one man.

My fader before my fader get him wife borku.*
E no' get equality palaver; he live well
For he be oga† for im own house.
But dat time done pass before the white man come
Wit 'im
    One wife for one man,

Tell me how una‡ woman no go make yanga§
Wen'e know say na'im only dey.
Suppose say – make God no 'gree – 'e no born at all?§§
A'tell you dat man bin dey crazy wey start
    One wife for one man.

Jus' tell me how one wife fit do one man;
How go fit stay all time for him house
For time when belleh done kommot.
How many pickin', self, one woman fit born
    Wen one wife be for one man?

---

* borku: plenty.
† oga: master or Lord.
‡ una: variation of 'your'.
§ yanga: vanity, pride, and perversity.
§§ she has no children.

Suppose, self, say no so-so woman your wife dey born
Suppose your wife sabe book, no'sabe make chop;
Den, how you go tell man make'e no' go out
Sake of dis divorce? Bo, dis culture na waya O!
    Wen one wife be for one man.

Okogbule Wonodi

Planting

Lights on the shore
that was our port,
that was our fort;

and wind swaying scenes
that we know
                    aside,
while the sea shells
stand aside,
season aside to make
mouths at us

birds on the stems,
pecking at the scare-crows
to call the farmer home,
who then shall follow,
with white shirts
the dance of his father
as tractors bite down
the yam god
and the squirrels skip about
making faces at us?

Stand
You that hate not
and praise not
these shifting scenes,
season and blow
the horn of *Rebisi*;*

* Rebisi: ancestral god of the Diobu people.

that we,
who shall hear
the cock at night
and see the red snake at day
and they that shall follow,
bow not
when the sea shells
season aside
making mouths at us.

Salute to Icheke

When did I cease to be
the bird that I have been;
was it that I have fallen
sullen at midstream,
or immersed earthwise
I have gone dusty with wives
that cook for men with irregularities
between their thighs?

    No father.
I am yet your harp;
tune me but fingerly
and my strings will echo
songs of my inside.

I am your right hand,
I will mend your barn
and girdle my breath
for after this harvest
there's the visit adults
and orphans will call
from windowless houses;
then will come the test
of my planting songs.

Michael Echeruo

Melting Pot

It is dark, now, and grave

This bowl of a world
That rings me round and round
And will not let me marvel enough
At this dull sky
At the ignorance of these men
Who cannot know what chance can do

I shudder
Before this bowl of a world,
At this dull sky.

Will they not, all of them,
Call me names when they hear
Their blind man of this city
Stumbled on an udara underfoot
And lost it in the search for more?

Wish they could see half
What my eyes see, or know
Half what I know!
The Century's blind man!

Man and God Distinguished

Man sees the stars
   and turns aside
   suspicious of such tidings
   on a perilous midnight.

Man turns his face
   from the terrors of incense
   for the tigers are howling
   when Man means to go home
   on a star-spangled midnight.

There can be no salt, and no joy
   from fresh dew in the morning,
   from wife or from home or from life
   in the wake of such tidings
   as stars and terrors of incense.

Afterwards, Man dies.

Sheets with the whiteness of stars
   and incense and oil and dirt
   and tongue knowing no spices, no salt.

And the cold angel caresses the God!

Femi Fatoba

In America

In America
  The highway runs too fast
    For men to feel the ground underneath;
      The mirage does not have time
        To look like water:
          And too many rainbows
          Strangle the clouds.

Those Lucky Few

I am one of those lucky few
Who have no sense of smell:

When the boss demands
And sleeps with my wife
Let her come home for a bath
And put on her best clothes,
A promotion party does not smell;

When the Honourable Minister lures my daughter
And silences me with a contract award
It is a father's reward
And it does not smell;

When I take my mother to the medicineman
For the money ritual
How do you expect me to remember
The smell of an umbilical cord
Severed years ago

Or that of the blood that binds
When I use my brother's skull
For AWURE* soap?

I do not smell
Little children's belch of hunger
When I snatch food from them
To feed my dog;

I am one of those lucky few
Who have lost the sense of smell.

Hooker

Many are the gods
Who guide the prostitute's feet
As she walks the cobblestones of sex:
The god of the bachelor
Made impotent by shyness
The god of the married man
Tired of his regular side of the bed
The god of the pimp
Who hopes in other men's desires
The god of the policeman
Whose vice is hidden under
The seat of the patrol car
The god of the magistrate
Who wields our common virtue
In his six-inch gavel
The catholic god of the priest
Lashing out with his olive branch of damnation
The god of the housewife
Whose husband neither talks in his sleep
Nor feels an after-effect.

* AWURE: a good-luck charm.

And you, the innocent
Cast your stone of prayer thus:
Let not an honest policeman
Be a black cat in her path
Let not the gold-sucking pimp
Scar her beyond plastic surgery
Let technology brace her bedposts
With the coldness of steel
And strengthen her mattress
With the suppleness of liquid muscles.

And this from me:
Lord, keep the moist heart
Always warm between her legs
Let her reap more than mere bubbles
From the froths of her shallow pool
Where men go to drown.

The Woman Who Wants to be My Wife

Were I not a man as men are,
Why ask for gourds of breasts
In the laps of harvest:

The woman
Who wants to be my wife
Inherited her father's chest:
She says:

> Who has ever heard of any man
> Feeding his children with the sugarcane
> Or wrinkled lemons in his loins:
> Let the pawpaw
> Wear her husband's manhood
> Like beads, for birds
> To peck and children to pluck.

Since bigness is the yam's only beauty
Shall we then lie in hope that
The farmer shall taste of sweet potatoes
Without kneeling to greet the Earth:

The woman
Who wants to be my wife
Inherited Ifa's tongue;
We shall sleep on
A chest of riddles and proverbs.

Pol N Ndu

udude
(at cock crow)

grave number twenty-four
red axe forged from last burials
of twenty three corpses in me:
Okpoko

horn-man call,
nude queens low in chant
far from lay-men
far from grasshoppers
trembling at your charged incantations:
Mmanwu

transmitting dead-land rumbles
in diction computed
at first cock-crow:
Udude

raw-material un-human
in invincible cocoon
explaining miracle photogropic:
burst-balloon

time-keeper of innumerable sperms
frantic in vibration
to chaotic chemistry:
I win!

The purest victory of all . . .
victory of vision
        of visitation
        of creation
perfect without contribution,
new-born fire-intricate
delicate because sharp
fierce in steadiness

I yearn

Evacuation

Distance
explodes
with cannon

Fire flakes
rain with
fire balls

the shrieking
the sleeping
the naked
the ragged
the clothed

melting
in the frenzy

weird things
herding nowhere

reset
the tents
in sulphur
or in sun

Onwuchekwa Jemie

Iroko

1

Old chronicler
landscape mirror without a memory
whose annals are the cipher
  of blood and earth
   tangled in your veins
seeing and waiting and saying nothing
silent as the desert sand —
who can discover the secrets of the iroko
   on the village square?

See here
shortlegged generation
striding from peak to peak
  past present
  from past to future
stand a moment and contemplate the iroko
apotheosis of the tense present
waiting
waiting for its date with the bulldozer

2

Come, labyrinth
knowledge makes us unhappy
the iroko tells us nothing

Toward a Poetics

1

The great dark work
                    has not yet been written
    a monument to our age
                        which is the age of negritude

It will be written by a pop artist
    who will dismember his contemporaries
            image by image
                        and phrase by phrase

and
        adding a touch of dung
                            a dash of dirt and corn
            will reassemble them
                        in a fierce startling
            collation

2

        To speak with a public voice
        the poet must be
                        angry with the world
            and the way it is
                        He must speak with rage
tempered by grandeur
                The sugarcandy school is not worth a line
                The prophets of doom offer nothing
                            but unreal visions
                    of strange places ruined
                            empty cupolas
                    void niches
                                vacant dais

and under the arches dust and scorpions
    in the vaults spiders
                rats
      wind broken-broken
        From a gloomy corner
            angels cart off
                    the coffin of God
      But you who have known no God
  but forests and waterfalls
          and the bitter sun
  you will articulate the totality
    the embarrassment
          pride
  despair
        and hope
           and never forget the hope
        of a continent in earthquake
You will speak
    of black and white
  and sometimes of red
      trisyllabic reality
        in which the earth is packed
  awful tricolour
    behind which the frightened spirit
            hides itself
   am reaching for
     a modern grand style
to lift me away
    words at a time
  from the colourless
        flat irony
          of life

Molara Ogundipe-Leslie

Song at the African Middle Class
(for Augustinho Neto)

we charge through the skies of disillusion,
seeking the widening of eyes, we gaze at chaos,
speak to deadened hearts and ears stopped with
commerce. We drift around our region of clowns,
walking on air as dreams fly behind some eyes,
some forage among broken bodies, fractured minds
to find just ways retraced and new like beaten cloth.

and if they come again
will they come again?
and if they come again
will they dance this time?
will the new egunguns dance once more
resplendent in rich-glassed cloths?
will they be of their people's needs,
rise to those needs, settle whirling rifts
salve, O, festering hearts?
will they say when they come
O my people, O my people, how to love you delicately?

Aig Higo

Ritual Murder

No animals will live
Rivers will be dry
The rotund seal will snap
Eager vultures will show
The sacred spring is stained red with lust

Our seedlings bake on the rocks
Fresh leaves wither in pain
The black-robed virgins ate here, hot-eyed,
Breathing agony, prowling with parted lips.

I hear their voodoo dance to soothe
And melt the hurt strains of their trance.
They've come to mourn the spectral eunuchs of the shrine.

Hidesong

     I struck tomorrow square in the face
Yesterday groaned and said,
         'Please mind your steps today.'
     I left them swimming with today.

       Hidesong
       Birdsong
       Unto my soul
       What funeral pyre rejects your bones?

My spider soul is spinning
Spinning
    Spinning endlessly.

Scarabwise I tow my days along
Alone I tow my death along.

Niyi Osundare

The Sand Seer

Let your wandering fingers
Trek in these sands
And open up the vista
To the mystery of time.

You cast no nuts
Fling no cords
Ring no bells
Nor seek yesterlives
At the root of graveyard turf.

Vista atoms of practised
eyes, seen everywhere
Knowing the secret of
Every toe. Truths lie
Undressed and the riddle
of the marrow is cracked
Upon a grain of sooth.

Let the sparkle of these
Sands telescope enigmatic
Time and catch the bird on
Tomorrow's tree.

       which woman makes best wife
       which profession makes richest
       men, what to do or undo that
       I may live till I please?

The future shrinks to eye-shot
As you sit there counting
Lots in grains of sand.

I Sing of Change

Sing on: somewhere, at some new moon,
We'll learn that sleeping is not death,
Hearing the whole earth change its tune.
                                    W. B. Yeats

I sing
of the beauty of Athens
without its slaves

Of a world free
of kings and queens
and other remnants
of an arbitrary past

Of earth
with no
sharp north
or deep south
without blind curtains
or iron walls

of the end
of warlords and armouries
and prisons of hate and fear

Of deserts treeing
and fruiting
after the quickening rains

Of the sun
radiating ignorance
and stars informing
nights of unknowing

I sing of a world reshaped

The Word

is a pod
quick with unspoken seeds
exploding in the dry season
of occasion

is an egg
broken,
it spreads
ungatherably

ear's food
mind's nurture
router of silences
sun of noons of action

Like the Bee
(after Francis Bacon)

Not like the spider
draping crowded rooms
in the wanton web
of flimsy looms
a welter of legs spinning
silky bridges, fragile,
for the empty feet of air

Not like the wood-insect
carpentering logs to fashion
its own prison
stockaded pupae peeping
behind bars of enslaving labour

But like the bee
brewing one honey
from the nectars
of several seasons
pleasing the bud
of every clime.

A Nib in the Pond

We read your lines
opening up the earth
like a book of paths
hear your voice
melting the wax of a thousand seasons

You who throw a nib
in the pond of silence
the ripples in your inkpot
convulse barracks and powerbrothels
overturning plots of plunder
lying on calculating tables
like poison bowls

We sing the lines
and hear our voice
read the words
and see ourselves
in the mirror of every letter

Now
though hands are two
we know which wipes the anus
there is a fork in the road
but we know the shorter way home.

Not Standing Still

I grew weary of the tyranny of water
and spat in the sea
I grew wary of the power of the sun
and lit candles at noon

A juicy rodent ran across
my morning path
I aimed my water-pot
at its teasing head
the quarry mocked
the potsherds of my lust
but it didn't go
without a dripping tail

Not standing still
is the beginning of battle
he will never pluck the fruit
whose back caresses the earth

The circle which has a beginning
also has an end
a little patience is what it needs
the stammerer will call
his father's name.

Funso Aiyejina

Let Us Remember
(for Dax, a fellow traveller)

We who have listened to silences abort
before they were diagnosed
as stream-flow of seminal blood
out of tune with monthly cycles . . .

we who have collected clouds
that eventually burst into storms
and left us aghast as our crops
became feeders to ocean bound streams . . .

we who can point to fragments of kites
and strands of thread
entangled on high voltage cables
as evidence of our dispersed dreams . . .

we who can smell the stench of dead pigeons
by the waterless fountains of our memorial squares
as evidence of the death of the *in*
in our independence . . .

we who have danced at festivals of arts
while cripples from new tribes
walk around on stilts and trample
our pre-harvest fields of crops to death . . .

let us remember
how men of parliament vacationed the electorate,
bandits demanded donations with which to refill
treasuries they had looted into family pots,
and power dissolved the people . . .

let us remember
how men, feline skunks, bury their insides sub rosa
forgetful of bamboo groves whose sacred flutes will grow
to play the tunes they plant into beachsand
and manifest the ugly lump on the king's crowned head
which he forbids his barber to proclaim before the people

May Ours Not Be

May ours not be like the story
of the Ear and the Mosquito;
but if it is, remember, o plunderers,
the Mosquito's eternal vow of protest,
for we shall become like lice
forever in your seams,
ant-heads that even in death
burrow deep into the flesh,
chameleon faeces that cannot
be wiped off the feet,
and regenerating earthworms
that multiply by their pieces;
if there is no rainbow in the sky,
we know to create one
by splashing water in the face of the sun;
if sleepers' hands protect their ears,
mosquitoes must learn to bite at their legs
to awaken them into their broken pledges;
if treasure hunters disturb our Orukwu rockhill,
thunder will break behind our tongues of lightning
like arrows in flight . . .

And What If They Broke Wind in Public?

Such was our veneration of age as wisdom
That when elders broke wind in public
Without hesitation, we named them patriots
Congratulated them for jobs well done
And wished them many more years of service.

Enthralled by their display of human frailty
And their experience of the future in the past
We camped at their feet, silent and willing eyes
Drinking our fill from pregnant wisdom gourds
Measured and served in intricate webs of words.

We grew to know that no matter how long it may take
The stammerer will give voice to his father's name;
The bastard, only the bastard points at his origin
Even though in ruins, with a sneering left finger;
No matter how dark, the black goat finds its trail home.

A View of a View
(for Ropo Sekoni)

From the babylonic heights
of a Lagos high rise hotel
with balconies overlooking dawn
(a silver canvas on the Atlantic),
my eyes threaded the horizon
to a fisherman in the distance
silent and erect in his dug-out
as he prepares to cast his net
before the arrival of trawlers,

patient and stoic, like death
waiting for the appropriate tide
to come ashore with the ultimate gift
for the hotel's resident five-star guests
(chameleons with wardrobes for all occasions)
whose coded lives are made purer and safer
by the equivocation of every official probe.

Odia Ofeimun

Let Them Choose Paths

They choose paths
who think there are paths to choose,
They make banners and float
our next republic.

They scour the garbage
of folklore
for the piece of silver
hidden by the wily tortoise.

They seek life
who cower at growths of lianas and creepers,
They run from the tangled stems
in search of stripped wisdom.

Pathfinders, all
they do not dare to know,
the thrill of building roads anew
too soft, too spiritless to stand
the course of sweat
down the smalls of their backs.

Let them choose paths
who think there are paths to choose.
We, we must grow new eyes
to see the asphalt in the chaste forest.

A Naming Day

Festive draperies override the claims of
bread and fresh air in this house

Gaudy buntings take breath away
from the newborn muffled in damask

in lace, in nameless riots of colours.
Mothers redress the loss of breast-milk

(so indecent to breast-feed children
now that mothers have turned mummies)

sorcerers of the supermarket conjuring
toys to people the lonesome hours
of unsung nurseries

Mothers have turned mummies
and growing up means to grind and wallow
in adult games of self-deceit
before the antimony of truth has time
to lay its fingers on the little heads

A Gong
(for Miriam Makeba)

Your voice awakens
the agony of brothers
drowned in their skokiaan tins
of pain

The naked virgin
from your limpid moon – out of
the dead sleep of children –
walks the thorned footpath
of my being

Is it all grief? –
this grey legend
of your night
gives birth to love, hope
gold landscapes
in tears and death

Is it mere sorcery? –
this rhythm swarms
with pagan tentacles upon moments
to baptize the world
with conscience,
and unfurl an aura of innocence

Black woman, you rouse in me a bestial joy
whetting a desire to fight
to plunder, if only to fulfil
the promise,
the gentle gleam of that Canaan
on your horizons

Break Me Out

Away from the sweated faces
the grimy masks of harried lovers
who forget their vows
sucked into the battled frenzy
of spinning plastic coins
father, break me out

Away from fallen mothers
who forget their heirs
in burning nurseries
cuddling paper money
with orgasmic relish
father, break me out

Break me out in the dead of night
before the early cockcrow saps my will
before the rumour of breakfast smells
topples my driving will

Break me out, I'm willing
though tethered by the ankle
to wistful longings, to mermaids
the lagoon vomits and swallows
in rude gasps, rude deceits

Do, break me out
far out of the whirldance
that ruins
the whirldance that ruined them
our bravest, our finest emissaries

They traded their wills to the wind
till their hearts dissolved in black gold
They traded their heads to the wind
till they lost the message of the gods

Father, break me out.

Ifi Amadiume

Bitter

If you were to squeeze me and wash,
squeeze me and wash,
squeeze and wash me,
and I foam,
again and again,
like bitter-leaf
left out too long to wither,
you would not squeeze
the bitterness out of me.

Iva Valley

Man of my mother's people,
in your hair of cotton wool,
I counted strands of wisdom untold.
In your eyes luminous,
I saw pearls
picked by my mother;
a naked beaded maiden
in silky black skin
running wild in Iva Valley.

Man of my mother's people,
in your brows
like garden ridges,
I saw the ancient fruits,

my mother, girlish,
lips cherry black,
eating nuts and berries
of Iva Valley.

Man of my mother's people,
in the strongness of your bones,
your aged body
firm and fatless,
I saw my mother
In lightness of limbs
as drops of water
from a pot
steady on her plaited head
made strings of gems
on her body
sensuous in camwood
as she walked the Iva Valley.

Man of the mother's people,
today as they put camphor
and perfumes foreign
on my mother's defrosted body,
as they put my mother
in coffin ghost-white,
man of my mother's people,
as I sought solace
in your sunken eyes
now as cold as the coal-tarred road
that carried my mother far away,
there were no berries
nor precious stones
only broken lorries
and bones of the dead
as we meandered past Milikin-Hill,
sitting oppressive
in dangerous modernity
on Iva Valley

and the heads of the ancient ones,
defiled in rust, petrol and blood.

Man of my mother's people,
they say Iva is like a woman
in incestuous pregnancy
her belly swollen with child;
her own flesh and blood –
her sons,
first Trade Unionists
grounded by the
heavy arms of exploiters
before they could walk,
their bodies,
ridden in white bullets,
were dumped into her,
as they sucked her blackblood,
vampire-like
for coal.

They say the veins of Iva
no longer run black
but red in blood;
the vampire has sunk its teeth elsewhere,
suckling black blood for oil.

You see,
man of my mother's people,
with stories strong
of roaming restless souls
in Iva Valley,
for fear of ghosts,
they have run round the corner
Nine Miles,
opened the bowels of the Earth
for a new road
to cut off Iva
now in labour.

But ghosts fly!

Ben Okri

The Incandescence of the Wind

The incandescence of the wind
bothers me
in this vineyard.
Is there a searing clarity
about the noises
rising daily
from this riverbed we call our own?

The yam-tubers bleed our sorrows.
Crows in the fields
scream of despair.
Machetes pollute our food
with rust.
The masters conduct their
plunderings
with quiet murders:
The victims perform maypole dances
around the village shrines.

There is a cold fire in the air.
I hear it
consume the groins
of heroes
and shrivel the guts
of martyrs.
The name of the fire
is printed on grave stones:
names squeezed from tubers of life
and collective cowardice.

At night mothers scream
of children lost in the city fires
of children lost in neon signs
and cellars of madness.
I hear noises from the streets:
men are lost in files
or have wandered
into the fractured severity
of military gun-shots
have become a generation
drenched in petrol
camp-fired
and barbecued
in the fevers
of elections
riots
coups.

The incandescence in the air
burns inward.
Is there a name for this fear?
Is there a fearful country
in these fields
where such realities are
manufactured whole?

I heard a secret
in the burning iron of the mornings.
Animals
have delivered eggs of blood.
Women
have discovered the secret
of an inviolable flesh-haze.
There are multiple deaths
in the riverbeds
and junkyards
polluting our world
with an irascible sense
of failure.

Shall we join them
or shall we celebrate
the vision of empty offices
the short-sightedness of power.

Break the bread
of initiation into
revolt:
We shall celebrate with our
emaciated chests.
We shall clench and raise our fists
in the wonder of incandescence.

I hear a light
bursting up through
the bright blue roots
and the yellow skeletons.
We have breathed
our self-love in those bones.
We have breathed
incantations
at those worms
that ravage our serenity.

The graveyards heave.
The riverbeds sigh.
And I wake surprised:
  – the incandescence has become
    our own
  – the skeletons have reclaimed
    the lands
  – a new spirit breathing phosphorous
    has grown
    into the blue roots of the times.

An African Elegy

We are the miracles that God made
To taste the bitter fruit of Time.
We are precious.
And one day our suffering
Will turn into the wonders of the earth.

There are things that burn me now
Which turn golden when I am happy.
Do you see the mystery of our pain?
That we bear poverty
And are able to sing and dream sweet things

And that we never curse the air when it is warm
Or the fruit when it tastes so good
Or the lights that bounce gently on the waters?
We bless things even in our pain.
We bless them in silence.

That is why our music is so sweet.
It makes the air remember.
There are secret miracles at work
That only Time will bring forth.
I too have heard the dead singing.

And they tell me that
This life is good
They tell me to live it gently
With fire, and always with hope.
There is wonder here

And there is surprise
In everything the unseen moves.
The ocean is full of songs.
The sky is not an enemy.
Destiny is our friend.

On Edge of Time Future

1

I remember the history well:
The soldiers and politicians emerged
With briefcases and guns
And celebrations on city nights.

They scoured the mess
Reviewed our history
Saw the executions at dawn
Then sighed with secret policemen

And decided something
Had to be done.

They scoured the mess
Resurrected old blue-prints
Of vicious times
Tracked the shapes of sinking cities

And learned at last
That nothing can be avoided
And so avoided everything.
I remember the history well.

2

We emerged from our rubbish mounds
Discovered a view of the sky
As the air danced in heat.

Through the view of the city
In flames, we rewound times
Of executions at beaches.
Salt streamed down our brows.

Everywhere stagger victims of rigged elections
Monolithic accidents on hungry roads
The infinite web of ethnic politics
Power-dreams and fevered winds.

The nation was a map stitched
From the grabbing of future flesh
And became a rush through
Historical slime.

3

We emerged on edge
Of time future
With bright fumes
From burning towers.

The fumes lit political rallies.
We started a war
Ended it
And dreamed about our chance.

Fat fish eat little fish
Big ones arrange executions
And armed robberies.
Our rubbish shapes us all.

I remember the history well.
The tiger's snarl is bought
In currencies of silence.
Eggs grow large:

A monstrous face is hatched.
On the edge of time future
I am a boy
With running sores

Of remembered history
Watching the stitches widen
Waiting for the volcano's laughter
In the fevered winds

Hearing the gnash
Of those who will join us
At the mighty gateways
With new blue-prints

With dew as seal
And fire as constant
And a trail through time past
To us

Who remember the history well.
We weave words on red
And sing on the edge of blue.
And with our nerves primed

We shall spin silk from rubbish
And frame time with our resolve.

And If You Should Leave Me

And if you should leave me
I would say that the ghost
Of Cassandra
Has passed through
My eyes
I would say that the stars
In their malice
Merely light up the sky
To stretch my torment
And that the waves crash
On the shores
To bring salt-stings on
My face:
For you re-connect me with
All the lights of the sky
And the salt of the waves
And the myths in the air.
And with your passing
The evening would become too dark
    To dream in
And the morning
    Too bright.

São Tomé

Alda do Espirito Santo

Where are the Men Seized in This Wind of Madness?

Blood falling in drops to the earth
men dying in the forest
and blood falling, falling . . .
on those cast into the sea . . .
Fernão Dias for ever in the story
of Ilha Verde, red with blood,
of men struck down
in the vast arena of the quay.
Alas the quay, the blood, the men,
the fetters, the lash of beatings
resound, resound, resound
dropping in the silence of prostrated lives
of cries, and howls of pain
from men who are men no more,
in the hands of nameless butchers.
Zé Mulato in the story of the quay
shooting men in the silence
of bodies falling.
Alas Zé Mulato, Zé Mulato,
The Victims cry for vengeance
The sea, the sea of Fernão Dias
devouring human lives
is bloody red.
– We are arisen –
Our eyes are turned to you.
Our lives entombed
in fields of death,

men of the Fifth of February
men fallen in the furnace of death
imploring pity
screaming for life,
dead without air, without water
they all arise
from the common grave
and upright in the chorus of justice
cry for vengeance . . .
    The fallen bodies in the forest,
the homes, the homes of men
destroyed in the gulf
of ravening fire,
lives incinerated,
raise the unaccustomed chorus of justice
crying for vengeance.
And all you hangmen
all you torturers
sitting in the dock:
— What have you done with my people? . . .
— What do you answer?
— Where is my people? . . .
And I answer in the silence
of voices raised
demanding justice . . .
One by one, through all the line . . .
For you, tormentors,
forgiveness has no name.
Justice shall be heard.
And the blood of lives fallen
in the forests of death,
innocent blood
drenching the earth
in a silence of terrors
shall make the earth fruitful,
crying for justice.

It is the flame of humanity
singing of hope
in a world without bonds
where liberty
is the fatherland of men . . .

Grandma Mariana

Grandma Mariana, washerwoman
for the whites in the Fazenda
One day she came from distant lands
with her piece of cloth round waist
and stayed.
Grandma Mariana stayed
washing, washing away, on the plantation
smoking her gourd pipe
outside the slave-quarters' door
remembering the journey from her sisal fields
on a sinister day
to the distant island
where the hard labour
erased the memory
of the bulls, the deaths,
away in the distant Cubal.

Grandma Mariana came
and sat outside the slave-quarters' door
and smoked her gourd pipe
washing, washing,
a wall of silence.

The years drained away
in the hot land.

– 'Grandma Mariana, Grandma Mariana
it is time to leave.
Go back to your vast lands
of endless plantations.'

– 'Where's the people's land?
Old woman comes, never returns . . .
I came from afar,
years and years spent in this yard . . .
Mad old woman does not have land anymore
I will stay here, silly boy.'

Grandma Mariana, smoking her gourd pipe
at the doorstep of your dark alley,
old little Grandma tell us
your inglorious story.
Live, vegetate
in the shade of the yard
you won't tell your story.

Grandma Mariana, my little Grandma,
smoking her gourd pipe
on the doorstep of the slave-quarters
you won't tell of your destiny . . .
Why did you cross the seas, old little grandma,
and remain here, all by yourself
smoking your gourd pipe?

Senegal

Léopold Sédar Senghor

In Memoriam

It is Sunday.
I fear the crowd of my brothers with stony faces.
From my tower of glass filled with pain, the nagging Ancestors
I gaze at roofs and hills in the fog
In the silence – the chimneys are grave and bare.
At their feet sleep my dead, all my dreams are dust
All my dreams, the liberal blood spills all along the streets, mixing
    with the blood of the butcheries.
And now, from this observatory as from a suburb
I watch my dreams float vaguely through the streets, lie at the hills'
    feet
Like the guides of my race on the banks of Gambia or Saloum,
Now of the Seine, at the feet of these hills.
Let me think of my dead!
Yesterday it was Toussaint, the solemn anniversary of the sun
And no remembrance in any cemetery.
Ah, dead ones who have always refused to die, who have known
    how to fight death
By Seine or Sine, and in my fragile veins pushed the invincible
    blood,
Protect my dreams as you have made your sons, wanderers on
    delicate feet.
Oh Dead, protect the roofs of Paris in the Sunday fog
The roofs which guard my dead
That from the perilous safety of my tower I may descend to the
    streets
To join my brothers with blue eyes
With hard hands.

Night of Sine

Woman, rest on my brow your balsam hands, your hands gentler
 than fur.
The tall palm trees swinging in the nightwind
Hardly rustle. Not even cradlesongs,
The rhythmic silence rocks us.
Listen to its song, listen to the beating of our dark blood, listen
To the beating of the dark pulse of Africa in the mist of lost
 villages.
Now the tired moon sinks towards its bed of slack water,
Now the peals of laughter even fall asleep, and the bards
 themselves
Dandle their heads like children on the backs of their mothers.
Now the feet of the dancers grow heavy and heavy grows the
 tongue of the singers.
This is the hour of the stars and of the night that dreams
And reclines on this hill of clouds, draped in her long gown of
 milk.
The roofs of the houses gleam gently. What are they telling so
 confidently to the stars?
Inside the hearth is extinguished in the intimacy of bitter and sweet
 scents.
Woman, light the lamp of clear oil, and let the children in bed talk
 about their ancestors, like their parents.
Listen to the voice of the ancients of Elissa. Like we, exiled,
They did not want to die, lest their seminal flood be lost in the
 sand.
Let me listen in the smoky hut for the shadowy visit of propitious
 souls.
My head on your breast glowing, like a kuskus ball smoking out of
 the fire,
Let me breathe the smell of our dead, let me contemplate and
 repeat their living voice, let me learn
To live before I sink, deeper than the diver, into the lofty depth of
 sleep.

Luxembourg 1939

This morning at the Luxembourg, this autumn at the Luxembourg,
    as I lived and relived my youth
No loafers, no water, no boats upon the water, no children, no
    flowers.
Ah! the September flowers and the sunburnt cries of children who
    defied the coming winter.
Only two old boys trying to play tennis.
This autumn morning without children – the children's theatre is
    shut!
This Luxembourg where I cannot trace my youth, those years fresh
    as the lawns.
My dreams defeated, my comrades despairing, can it be so?
Behold them falling like leaves with the leaves, withered and
    wounded trampled to death the colour of blood
To be shovelled into what common grave?
I do not know this Luxembourg, these soldiers mounting guard.
They have put guns to protect the whispering retreat of Senators,
They have cut trenches under the bench where I first learnt the
    soft flowering of lips.
That notice again! Ah yes, dangerous youth!
I watch the leaves fall into the shelters, into the ditches, into the
    trenches
Where the blood of a generation flows.
Europe is burying the yeast of nations and the hope of newer
    races.

Blues

The spring has swept the ice from all my frozen rivers
My young sap trembles at the first caresses along the tender bark.
But see how in the midst of July I am blinder than the Arctic
    winter!
My wings beat and break against the barriers of heaven

No ray pierces the deaf vault of my bitterness.
What sign is there to find? What key to strike?
And how can god be reached by hurling javelins?
Royal Summer of the distant South, you will come too late, in a
	hateful September!
In what book can I find the thrill of your reverberation?
And on the pages of what book, on what impossible lips taste your
	delirious love?

The impatient fit leaves me. Oh! the dull beat of the rain on the
	leaves!
Just play me your 'Solitude', Duke, till I cry myself to sleep.

Prayer to Masks

Black mask, red mask, you black and white masks,
Rectangular masks through whom the spirit breathes,
I greet you in silence!
And you too, my lionheaded ancestor.
You guard this place, that is closed to any feminine laughter, to any
	mortal smile.
You purify the air of eternity, here where I breathe the air of my
	fathers.
Masks of markless faces, free from dimples and wrinkles,
You have composed this image, this my face that bends over the
	altar of white paper.
In the name of your image, listen to me!
Now while the Africa of despotism is dying – it is the agony of a
	pitiable princess
Like that of Europe to whom she is connected through the navel –
Now fix your immobile eyes upon your children who have been
	called
And who sacrifice their lives like the poor man his last garment
So that hereafter we may cry 'here' at the rebirth of the world
	being the leaven that the white flour needs.
For who else would teach rhythm to the world that has died of
	machines and cannons?

For who else should ejaculate the cry of joy, that arouses the dead
    and the wise in a new dawn?
Say, who else could return the memory of life to men with a torn
    hope?
They call us cotton heads, and coffee men, and oily men,
They call us men of death.
But we are the men of the dance whose feet only gain power when
    they beat the hard soil.

Visit

I dream in the intimate semi-darkness of an afternoon.
I am visited by the fatigues of the day,
The deceased of the year, the souvenirs of the decade,
Like the procession of the dead in the village on the horizon of the
    shallow sea.
It is the same sun bedewed with illusions,
The same sky unnerved by hidden presences,
The same sky feared by those who have a reckoning with the dead.
And suddenly my dead draw near to me . . .

What Dark Tempestuous Night

What dark tempestuous night has been hiding your face?
And what claps of thunder frighten you from the bed
When the fragile walls of my breast tremble?
I shudder with cold, trapped in the dew of the clearing.
O, I am lost in the treacherous paths of the forest.
Are these creepers or snakes that entangle my feet?
I slip into the mudhole of fear and my cry is suffocated in a watery
    rattle.
But when shall I hear your voice again, happy luminous morn?
When shall I recognize myself again in the laughing mirror of eyes,
    that are large like windows?
And what sacrifice will pacify the white mask of the goddess?

Perhaps the blood of chickens or goats, or the worthless blood in
　　my veins?
Or the prelude of my song, the ablution of my pride?

Give me propitious words.

New York
(for jazz orchestra: trumpet solo)

I

New York! At first I was confused by your beauty, by those great
　　golden long-legged girls.
So shy at first before your blue metallic eyes, your frosted smile
So shy. And the anguish in the depths of skyscraper streets
Lifting eyes hawkhooded to the sun's eclipse.
Sulphurous your light and livid the towers with heads that
　　thunderbolt the sky
The skyscrapers which defy the storms with muscles of steel and
　　stone-glazed hide.
But two weeks on the bare sidewalks of Manhattan
– At the end of the third week the fever seizes you with the
　　pounce of a leopard
Two weeks without rivers or fields, all the birds of the air
Falling sudden and dead on the high ashes of flat rooftops.
No smile of a child blooms, his hand refreshed in my hand,
No mother's breast, but only nylon legs. Legs and breasts that have
　　no sweat nor smell.
No tender word for there are no lips, only artificial hearts paid for
　　in hard cash
And no book where wisdom may be read. The painter's palette
　　blossoms with crystals of coral.
Nights of insomnia oh nights of Manhattan! So agitated by
　　flickering lights, while motor-horns howl of empty hours
And while dark waters carry away hygienic loves, like rivers flooded
　　with the corpses of children.

2

Now is the time of signs and reckonings
New York! Now is the time of manna and hyssop.
You must but listen to the trombones of God, let your heart beat
     in the rhythm of blood, your blood.
I saw in Harlem humming with noise with stately colours and
     flamboyant smells
– It was teatime at the house of the seller of pharmaceutical
     products –
I saw them preparing the festival of night for escape from the day.
I proclaim night more truthful than the day.
It was the pure hour when in the streets God makes the life that
     goes back beyond memory spring up
All the amphibious elements shining like suns.
Harlem Harlem! Now I saw Harlem! A green breeze of corn
     springs up from the pavements ploughed by the naked feet of
     dancers
Bottoms waves of silk and sword-blade breasts, water-lily ballets
     and fabulous masks.
At the feet of police-horses roll the mangoes of love from low
     houses.
And I saw along the sidewalks streams of white rum streams of
     black milk in the blue fog of cigars.
I saw the sky in the evening snow cotton-flowers and seraphims'
     wings and sorcerers' plumes.
Listen New York! Oh listen to your male voice of brass vibrating
     with oboes, the anguish choked with tears falling in great clots
     of blood
Listen to the distant beating of your nocturnal heart, rhythm and
     blood of the tom-tom, tom-tom blood and tom-tom.

3

New York! I say to you: New York let black blood flow into your
     blood
That it may rub the rust from your steel joints, like an oil of life,

That it may give to your bridges the bend of buttocks and the
    suppleness of creepers.
Now return the most ancient times, the unity recovered, the
    reconciliation of the Lion the Bull and the Tree
Thought linked to act, ear to heart, sign to sense.
There are your rivers murmuring with scented crocodiles and
    mirage-eyed manatees. And no need to invent the Sirens.
But it is enough to open the eyes to the rainbow of April
And the ears, above all the ears, to God who out of the laugh of a
    saxophone created the heaven and the earth in six days.
And the seventh day he slept the great sleep of the Negro.

You Held the Black Face
(for Khalam)

You held the black face of the warrior between your hands
Which seemed with fateful twilight luminous.
From the hill I watched the sunset in the bays of your eyes.
When shall I see my land again, the pure horizon of your face?
When shall I sit at the table of your dark breasts?
The nest of sweet decisions lies in the shade.
I shall see different skies and different eyes,
And shall drink from the sources of other lips, fresher than
    lemons,
I shall sleep under the roofs of other hair, protected from storms.
But every year, when the rum of spring kindles the veins afresh,
I shall mourn anew my home, and the rain of your eyes over the
    thirsty savannah.

I Will Pronounce Your Name
(for Tama)

I will pronounce your name, Naëtt, I will declaim you, Naëtt!
Naëtt, your name is mild like cinnamon, it is the fragrance in which
    the lemon grove sleeps,

Naëtt, your name is the sugared clarity of blooming coffee trees
And it resembles the savannah, that blossoms forth under the
    masculine ardour of the midday sun.
Name of dew, fresher than shadows of tamarind,
Fresher even than the short dusk, when the heat of the day is
    silenced.
Naëtt, that is the dry tornado, the hard clasp of lightning
Naëtt, coin of gold, shining coal, you my night, my sun! . . .
I am your hero, and now I have become your sorcerer, in order to
    pronounce your names.
Princess of Elissa, banished from Futa on the fateful day.

Be Not Amazed

Be not amazed beloved, if sometimes my song grows dark,
If I exchange the lyrical reed for the Khalam or the tama
And the green scent of the ricefields, for the swiftly galloping war
    drums.
I hear the threats of ancient deities, the furious cannonade of the
    god.
Oh, tomorrow perhaps, the purple voice of your bard will be silent
    for ever.
That is why my rhythm becomes so fast, that the fingers bleed on
    the Khalam.
Perhaps, beloved, I shall fall tomorrow, on a restless earth
Lamenting your sinking eyes, and the dark tom-tom of the mortars
    below.
And you will weep in the twilight for the glowing voice that sang
    your black beauty.

Birago Diop

Diptych

The Sun hung by a thread
In the depths of the Calabash dyed indigo
Boils the great Pot of Day.
Fearful of the approach of the Daughters of fire
The Shadow squats at the feet of the faithful.
The savannah is bright and harsh
All is sharp, forms and colours.
But in the anguished Silences made by Rumours
Of tiny sounds, neither hollow nor shrill,
Rises a ponderous Mystery,
A Mystery muffled and formless
Which surrounds and terrifies us.

The dark Loincloth pierced with nails of fire
Spread out on the Earth covers the bed of Night.
Fearful at the approach of the Daughters of shadow
The dog howls, the horse neighs
The Man crouches deep in his house.
The savannah is dark,
All is black, forms and colours
And in the anguished Silences made by Rumours
Of tiny sounds infinite or hollow or sharp
The tangled Paths of the Mystery
Slowly reveal themselves
For those who set out
And for those who return.

Vanity

If we tell, gently, gently
All that we shall one day have to tell,
Who then will hear our voices without laughter,
Sad complaining voices of beggars
Who indeed will hear them without laughter?

If we cry roughly of our torments
Ever increasing from the start of things,
What eyes will watch our large mouths
Shaped by the laughter of big children
What eyes will watch our large mouths?

What heart will listen to our clamouring?
What ear to our pitiful anger
Which grows in us like a tumour
In the black depth of our plaintive throats?

When our Dead come with their Dead
When they have spoken to us with their clumsy voices;
Just as our ears were deaf
To their cries, to their wild appeals
Just as our ears were deaf
They have left on the earth their cries,
In the air, on the water, where they have traced their signs
For us, blind deaf and unworthy Sons
Who see nothing of what they have made
In the air, on the water, where they have traced their signs.

And since we did not understand our dead
Since we have never listened to their cries
If we weep, gently, gently
If we cry roughly of our torments
What heart will listen to our clamouring,
What ear to our sobbing hearts?

Ball

A scroll of blue, an exquisite thought
Moves upwards in a secret accord
And the gentle pink explosion the shade filters
Drowns a woman's perfume in a heavy regret.

The languorous lament of the saxophone
Counts a string of troubles and vague promises
And, jagged or monotonous, its raucous cry
Sometimes awakes a desire I had thought dead.

Stop jazz, you scan the sobs and tears
That jealous hearts keep only to themselves.
Stop your scrap-iron din. Your uproar
Seems like a huge complaint where consent is born.

Viaticum

In one of the three pots
the three pots to which on certain evenings
the happy souls return
the serene breath of the ancestors,
the ancestors who were men,
the forefathers who were wise,
Mother wetted three fingers,
three fingers on her left hand:
the thumb, the index and the next;
I too wetted three fingers,
three fingers of my right hand:
the thumb, the index and the next.

With her three fingers red with blood,
with dog's blood,
with bull's blood,
with goat's blood,
Mother touched me three times.

She touched my forehead with her thumb,
With her index my left breast
And my navel with her middle finger.
I too held my fingers red with blood,
with dog's blood.
with bull's blood,
with goat's blood.
I held my three fingers to the winds
to the winds of the North, to the winds of the Levant,
to the winds of the South, to the winds of the setting sun;
and I raised my three fingers towards the Moon,
towards the full Moon, the Moon full and naked
when she rested deep in the largest pot.
Afterwards I plunged my three fingers in the sand
in the sand that had grown cold.
Then Mother said, 'Go into the world, go!
They will follow your steps in life.'

Since then I go
I follow the pathways
the pathways and roads
beyond the sea and even farther,
beyond the sea and beyond the beyond;
And whenever I approach the wicked,
the Men with black hearts,
whenever I approach the envious,
the Men with black hearts
before me moves the Breath of the Ancestors.

David Diop

Listen Comrades

Listen comrades of the struggling centuries
To the keen clamour of the Negro from Africa to the Americas
They have killed Mamba
As they killed the seven of Martinsville
Or the Madagascan down there in the pale light on the prisons
He held in his look comrades
The warm faith of a heart without anguish
And his smile despite agony
Despite the wounds of his broken body
Kept the bright colours of a bouquet of hope
It is true that they have killed Mamba with his white hairs
Who ten times poured forth for us milk and light
I feel his mouth on my dreams
And the peaceful tremor of his breast
And I am lost again
Like a plant torn from the maternal bosom
But no
For there rings out higher than my sorrows
Purer than the morning where the wild beast wakes
The cry of a hundred people smashing their cells
And my blood long held in exile
The blood they hoped to snare in a circle of words
Rediscovers the fervour that scatters the mists
Listen comrades of the struggling centuries
To the keen clamour of the Negro from Africa to the Americas
It is the sign of the dawn
The sign of brotherhood which comes to nourish the dreams of
    men.

Your Presence

In your presence I rediscovered my name
My name that was hidden under the pain of separation
I rediscovered the eyes no longer veiled with fever
And your laughter like a flame piercing the shadows
Has revealed Africa to me beyond the snows of yesterday
Ten years my love
With days of illusions and shattered ideas
And sleep made restless with alcohol
The suffering that burdens today with the taste of tomorrow
And that turns love into a boundless river
In your presence I have rediscovered the memory of my blood
And necklaces of laughter hung around our days
Days sparkling with ever new joys.

The Renegade

My brother you flash your teeth in response to every hypocrisy
My brother with gold-rimmed glasses
You give your master a blue-eyed faithful look
My poor brother in immaculate evening dress
Screaming and whispering and pleading in the parlours of
        condescension
We pity you
Your country's burning sun is nothing but a shadow
On your serene 'civilized' brow
And the thought of your grandmother's hut
Brings blushes to your face that is bleached
By years of humiliation and bad conscience
And while you trample on the bitter red soil of Africa
Let these words of anguish keep time with your restless step –
Oh I am lonely so lonely here.

Africa

Africa my Africa
Africa of proud warriors in ancestral savannahs
Africa of whom my grandmother sings
On the banks of the distant river
I have never known you
But your blood flows in my veins
Your beautiful black blood that irrigates the fields
The blood of your sweat
The sweat of your work
The work of your slavery
The slavery of your children
Africa tell me Africa
Is this you this back that is bent
This back that breaks under the weight of humiliation
This back trembling with red scars
And saying yes to the whip under the midday sun
But a grave voice answers me
Impetuous son that tree young and strong
That tree there
In splendid loveliness amidst white and faded flowers
That is Africa your Africa
That grows again patiently obstinately
And its fruit gradually acquires
The bitter taste of liberty.

The Vultures

In those days
When civilization kicked us in the face
When holy water slapped our cringing brows
The vultures built in the shadow of their talons
The bloodstained monument of tutelage
In those days

There was painful laughter on the metallic hell of the roads
And the monotonous rhythm of the paternoster
Drowned the howling on the plantations
O the bitter memories of extorted kisses
Of promises broken at the point of a gun
Of foreigners who did not seem human
Who knew all the books but did not know love
But we whose hands fertilize the womb of the earth
In spite of your songs of pride
In spite of the desolate villages of torn Africa
Hope was preserved in us as in a fortress
And from the mines of Swaziland to the factories of Europe
Spring will be reborn under our bright steps.

Annette M'Baye d'Erneville

Kassacks
to Ousmane, my son

You are a man, tonight!
You are a man, my son!
  By your bruised flesh
  By your spilled blood
  By your cold glance
  By your immobile thigh.

And your mother remembers
  Her night of love
  Her torn entrails
  Her silent groans
  Her open loins
  The envious looks of her wicked rivals
  The greedy suction of your flower-shaped mouth
The miraculous amulet that
– With the help of Allah –
Has guided your steps to this happy day.

You are a man, tonight!
You are a man, my son!
  By the cutting blade

  By your tried sex
  By your suppressed fear
  By the land of the Ancestors
Gawolo! . . . sing of this new man.
Young girls with upright breasts
Cry out his name to the wind.
Selbe N'Diaye, make this little man dance.

You are a man, my son.
You are a man tonight
They are all here:
   Those of your first moon
   Those you call fathers.
Look, look at them well;
They alone are the guardians of the earth
Of the earth that drank your blood.

Thierno Seydou Sall

Sugar Daddy

You come to me, promising
To comb out my white hair
I leave you all my wealth
Claiming your body in return.
I caress you, and you tell all
who care to hear;
'When my daddy comes, all
my contradictions will be resolved.'
Since then it's been a whole parade of problems
Tomorrow a baptism, tonight a death, at dawn
a marriage.
Without lamenting, I gave you all I possess
Knowing that you lie to me
I decided to give you no more money and you
accepted my blackmail and lay with me.
You tell everybody that I'm your
daddy and not your lover. Our bed
knows the truth.
Young girls, leave the old alone
they have discovered all your tricks in their
smallest particulars.

Amadou Elimane Kane

Violence

Images
From elsewhere
Have drunk
Your thoughts
Mortified
Your glance
Stitched up your tongue

Images
From elsewhere
Have forced you
To deny
yourself
To your own images

Images
From elsewhere
Have tied up
Your mind
And put you
To sleep
In the bed
Of self-destruction.

The Continent That Exists No More

I was walking through distant ages
  When I arrived in a continent
    Which perhaps had not existed
    Save to a distorted gaze

I was walking in a continent
  So far in the past
    That alienated eyes
      Could see it no more
And that the mercantilists had
Utterly caricatured

I walked in a continent
  Where every house
    Communicated with the cliffs
      The trees
      And the sacred streams

I walked in a remote continent
  Whose people banished the third part of things
    And their looks saw nothing
      But the words of love
      The words of solidarity

    The people of this continent
Lived only for poetic dreams
    Only for calm looks
    For looks filled with light

I was walking in a continent
  Where the women were queens
Where people could still conjugate their verbs
  Breathe
  Inspire
  Love one another
  And live

Without imperfection
  Without future

And without words found
Only in truncated dictionaries

I was walking in a continent
Where everyone offered their riches
   Their ears
   Their looks
   Their smiles

I was walking in a continent
   Whose people were not
      Slaves of money
They absorbed the beauties of nature
      In the temples of their dreams
         Washed free of all lying dust

Testament

I will weave for you, Astou, my princess
A lappa of rays in the depths of my calabash,
And dig in the most creative corner of my words,
   Far from appearances and leaden glances
A pyramid of joy, of plaited light
Where you will free yourself, a woven papyrus.

With my fertile heart, nourished by a pure ray
   Totally keyed to original rhymes
I will make for your gaze an infinite calabash
I know how to weave you a cloth of lunar rays
   Which will enfold you and brighten you
      To dodge the whole human comedy
         Come then!
The pyramid is your sacred place.

Sierra Leone

Syl Cheney-Coker

Six poems from *The Graveyard Also Has Teeth* (1980)

On Being a Poet in Sierra Leone

A poet alone in my country
I am seeking the verisimilitudes in life
the fire of metaphors the venom of verse
my country you are my heart living like a devastated landscape
always the magic of being underground of burying truth
of shedding your metaphysical form
country I wish to die being your poet
I who have so condemned and sold you
I who have so loved and hated you
imagine my sadness, the poetry of being you
a colossus strangled by fratricidal parasites
have I betrayed you writing my hermetic poetry
I suffer the estrangement of being too 'intellectual'
at the university the professors talk about the poetry
of Syl Cheney-Coker condemning students
to read me in the English honours class
my country I do not want that!
do not want to be cloistered in books alone
I want to be the albatross learning and living your fits
I want only to plough your fields
to be the breakfast of the peasants who read
to help the fishermen bring in their catch
I want to be your national symbol of life
because my heart is heavy country and exile calls
beating the pangs of oblivion on my brow

I want once more like the common man
to love a woman without dying of love
to leave a son or daughter to remember my grave
country you my pain, my phoenix, my disastrous gloating python
in whose belly all my anger dies
I am going to be happy to stop carrying my pain
like a grenade in my heart, I want to be simple
if possible to live with you, and then one day die leaving
my poetry, an imperfect metaphor of life!

Poem for a Guerrilla Leader
(to Amilcar Cabral)

Solitude supporting solitude on two pergolas
sunset shaping summer where the jungle closes in
man eating roots leaning on the theories of Fanon
it was there in his shadow that I saw the primordium of Africa

slaves supporting treachery behind sweet fraternal looks
minions of the bourgeoisie mingled with serfs
I know it all in serpentine bliss
feeling the tongues of fire obfuscating my life
cheek to cheek with that man in his solitude
murdered in his finest hour
by fratricidal negroes, brothers of lust!

to speak of his name I shed my sorrow
near this sea tormenting my memory with the cargoes of black
    flesh
bought with what portuguese asientos
sacred to the delight of the pope?
Ah when the journey was long sweetening the pain
my destiny to be born a slave enriching these brothers
who eat the flesh of wild boars . . .
my sadness knows it all piercing my heart!

and now the defoliated island rises colourless
the grass is the hands of those maimed by napalm
man-child leaping over the mutilated soul shouting
mother I am going away to be a revolutionary
to remake my brother I heard saying
O island O field you Cape Verde daughter in spoilage.

The Hunger of the Suffering Man

Sweating between his fingers, the agricultural man
sweating in his thorax the musician
sweating in his lungs the miner
sweating in his nausea the existential man
sweating in his refugee camp the Palestinian
driven out by the Jew who has forgotten Auschwitz
sweating in his ghetto the blackman
sweating in his carapace the animal-man
sweating when he escapes the innocent man
sweating in their duodena the children
battling the pigs on the garbage dump
sweating the woman whose urgent sex
brings me my brief joy
sweating the poor man whose house starves between the thighs
sweating the deadman, the marginal man
who wants his bones enamelled in gold
sweating the poor who died from the too, too rich
sweating the bronze man who suffers them all
sweating I who sing them!

Poem for a Lost Lover
(to Merle Alexander)

Eyes of heavenly essence, O breasts of the purity of breasts
Russian sapphire of the blue of eyes
O wine that mellows like the plenitude of Bach
Sargassian sea that is the calm of your heart
the patience of you loving my fragile soul
the courage of you moulding my moody words
I love you woman gentle in my memory!

O woman of the thirst of Siddhartha's love
you that I lost in the opium of my youth
have you fallen among the rocks off the New England coast
or now in premature grey nurse a stubborn tear
at the window watching winter's snow-coated leaves
here the tropical blossom of an African November
breathes gently on the tree of my heart
Oh that you could have known it woman of the sexual waters
heart of the spirit born of that love
dressing continents with garlands for whom I say
night strike my heart with the purest verse!

Letter to a Tormented Playwright
(for Yulisa Amadu Maddy)

Amadu I live alone inside four walls of books
some I have read others will grow cobwebs
or maybe like some old friends and lovers
will fade away with their undiscovered logic

the world that I have seen: New York
where I suffered the suicidal brother
and London where I discovered Hinostroza
Delgado, Ortega, Heraud and the other
Andean poets with a rage very much like ours!

remember Amadu how terrible I said it was
that you were in exile and working
in the Telephone Office in touch with all
the languages of the world but with no world
to call your own; how sad you looked that winter
drinking your life and reading poetry with me
in the damp chilly English coffee shops

*

remember I said how furious I was
that Vallejo had starved to death in Paris
that Rabéarivelo had killed himself
suffocated by an imaginary France
and I introduced Neruda and Guillen to you
and how in desperation we sought solace in the house
of John La Rose, that courageous Trinidadian poet

Amadu I am writing to you from the dungeon of my heart
the night brings me my grief and I am passive
waiting for someone to come, a woman
a friend, someone to soothe my dying heart!

now the memory of our lives brings a knife to my poems
our deaths which so burdened the beautiful Martiniquan
you said made you happy, she made you so happy, you a
      tormented playwright

*

sadness returns, the apparitions of my brothers
and my mother grows old thinking about them
and also seeing so much sadness in me her living and dying son
my mother who wishes me happy, who wants me to relive the son
she lost to poetry like a husband a wife to a trusted friend

but already the walls are closing around me
the rain has stopped and once again I am alone
waiting for them, the politicians of our country to come for me
to silence my right to shouting poetry loud in the parks
but who can shut up the rage the melodrama of being Sierra Leone
the farce of seeing their pictures daily in the papers

the knowledge of how though blindfolded and muzzled
something is growing, bloating, voluptuous and not despairing
I say to you for now, I embrace you brother.

The Road to Exile Thinking of Vallejo

Like others I get drunk in my blood
hiccuping and await the souls of my brothers
perennially on the song composed by the heliotrope heart
at midstream where the spirits walk
undisturbed!
excellent then, this sudden shower of locusts
expanse of cortege and the two roads
of the cemetery where time has its teeth
in the flesh of a mother who oxidizes her soul
with the waters of the passion-flower
as May is a brother just as October was a brother
linked to the prodigal who declares:

Mother I want to return into exile to be your poet!

hearing this, my mother seized by an element of nature
wondering whether I am going or staying seeing the roads
in my eyes, turns a terra-cotta sister and her hair
once black illuminates the night with its premature whiteness
my mother prevents my flight into myself
speaking to me through her silence through the beat of her heart
being that she loves me that she is always herself double
the sword fighting my days the lamp lighting my nights
when my heart sinks deep in the oasis
of its pain! she rejuvenates me calling back the me
that has died tracing the man-child to the poet
without understanding the dictates of my soul

*

blood absent from my soul my dog-starved days
on the peninsula of my Sierra Leone
my legacies which I counted in five carcasses

dancing drunk in the terrible summers
and that cruel winter polyphonic in verse

when I loved that woman without first learning how to live
I bled one night shedding poems from my heart!

It is recorded then: I'll die in exile!
thinking of my Sierra Leone
this country which has made me a poet
this country which has honoured me
with the two knives of my death passed crisscross
through my heart
so that I can say to a bleeding mother:

Mother I am returning into exile to be your poet!

Three poems from The Blood in the Desert's Eyes (1990)

The Philosopher

Who lived here when the stones were green
verdigris of age when the reptilians marched like men
into the night before that morning the sea
emptying its cup of wounds like a chasm of revolt.
like a castaway an old man kept his books in a cave
desolate his memory of life a portrait
like an abstraction of years, he lived
forgotten by others before the last tidal wave
I consecrate him seer his beard was a white book
where we read about kings and prophets
planners of the ruins astride our stormy conscience
to write what history the moon already dripping its sea of red
        blood

the whirlwind that licked over your body
amulet of season playing fangs on the translucent word
flagellant at crossroads where the word was nailed
neologist who dressed the world in hendecasyllabic verse

O monk saddened when you consecrated the word in body
stripped when you meditated in penury

you return shadow from shadow the word
transformed into phoenix you return the man
reigning the length of the raised cross
violated your soul we fashion you into memory
drift of a cyclone, man with whom we raise our conscience
you rise from your body to be equal to your name!

The Tin Gods

Watching the tombs tonight
the desert raises its shadow the desert
sees the caravan along its own arm:
playing this game of words the desert fights
over each word the sound of the noun
the ink on the scribe's page forgetting
the trail taken by the twin mules;
the desert's path is like two vessels
from a fountain consecrated by God
because the man who cried at the wailing wall
is brother of the man driven out of Palestine

prelude to an oasis of blood, I write
these lines against the book they quote
to silence the voice from the minaret
I write thinking of those who say at daggers drawn
to talk to the diplomats gives fresh baptism
to the music of Wagner

blood flows from the Litani
blood flows in Elait, in Sidon
where the white dove is strangled in its flight
and where the wandering Bedouin in search of his brother
the Jew is corralled because already the tin gods
drink the blood of the vineyard before the ripe harvest!

The Brotherhood of Man

The locomotive breaks its run
you descend to adjust your gaze
your century, looking through your narrow point
back into the Australopithecus grove, where, starting,
we hurried to arrive, naïve pleadings, into the rush of age

pagan journey I could tell, when this heart
begins to beat, was no sooner contemplated
before these crevices in my face marked my time
for the poet is he who travels everlastingly
embracing his neighbour embracing his enemy
to love life more to hate death less
in the red evenings the taste of fate
already salting my wounds with regret

goodnight, let us say farewell before we cry
so that when the fireflies dance round our shadows
nothing would remain but this grove where we ate
the primeval meal before leaving the warm cluster of love
for this cold taste of fate, this glacial world
this night, the locomotive continuing its run
into the never-ending day when I shall embrace tearfully my
    enemy.

Lemuel Johnson

Magic

Othello: Come, Desdemona. I have but an hour . . .

The quick straddle will do.
  for now.

nakedness itself is not the point; remember
this that *she hath eyes, and she chose me.*
they will have me loaded
otherwise, with injury and exclusion

in Venice; they will have me dead
on time for this their cousin and daughter
this my wife, *look to your wife* Iago says
and whispers *wear your eyes well* to do so.
I know he bends low, beyond all
consideration of boundary and home.

here, then, where we most live,
the two of us,
I pull myself in to the very tailbone,
attached as we are to the poisonous
fondness of kinship and fools.

Hagar, or, the Insufficiency of Metaphor

> such grief might make mountains stop
> reverse the waters where they flow
> Anna Akhmatova, 'Dedication'

I go, because you say nothing.

heavy in the mouth
the dead meat that weighs
heavy in your mouth
now is my tongue

move, if you are still, if,
that is, you will still
make me move.

in a short while, you will say
nothing important, no matter how

secretly tied to the bottom of eternity
to the austere touch that is to come:
the one that fears nothing irreparable

when last seen;
that centre was always nothing but a dot,
   and it wears out, now,
in the unlikelihood of being, myself,
ever the centre of yourself;

or of some god's late turn
to trade and traffic
and windstorm and sentence.

something grows and grows
raw in my very throat.

if you are still, move.
before you say another nothing.

The Defiance of Figures in Wood

Nana, what about love?
Love? . . . Love? . . . Love is not safe.
      Ama Ata Aidoo, 'Changes'

But barter we did: it remains still
to be clear what we won; what else
it was we lost:
whitefrocked girls on silly sundays
   in their yellow shoes;
small bottles and april showers;
the regent slant and tilt of a straw hat;
long-stockinged scriptures; the litter
of harbours where certain ladies once sat
on the railings of deserted quays and ate
out of the empty thighs of strange men

(wherever it was that cunt met dick
in the simple enough english
that jigs so at the heart of the matter).

like to like, and organizing chaos,
how could we sink?

the gods stand up for bastards:
in their own odd dance
they fall out of the sky,
with their foreskins peeled back.

we could kneel, too, on the sea,
ambitious as salt water
itself, and not sink; though the caked
hulls of ships, their ships,
when they depart, shake
the wakes we intend, or keep.

gravel, shale; compost heap or rock
face – and the earth thinks to reject
knowledge of our weight,
now that we know to pass yellow water
through the holes we are left to own;

we who had thought to hoard thought
in graceless aims,
diving for the difference
in some broken language of love!

call us Ishmael (if you please) or Barabbas;
Habibatu and Zenobia. Cain, too.
we take a count in figure and in sum,
no matter how hissed as injury into the ear;
we barter coinage for coin, and do not sink.

South Africa

Dennis Brutus

At a Funeral

(for Valencia Majombozi, who died shortly after qualifying as a doctor)

Black, green and gold at sunset: pageantry
And stubbled graves Expectant, of eternity,
In bride's-white, nun's-white veils the nurses gush their bounty
Of red-wine cloaks, frothing the bugled dirging slopes
Salute! Then ponder all this hollow panoply
For one whose gifts the mud devours, with our hopes.

Oh all you frustrate ones, powers tombed in dirt,
Aborted, not by Death but carrion books of birth
Arise! The brassy shout of Freedom stirs our earth;
Not Death but death's-head tyranny scythes our ground
And plots our narrow cells of pain defeat and dearth:
Better that we should die, than that we should lie down.

Nightsong: City

Sleep well, my love, sleep well:
the harbour lights glaze over restless docks,
police cars cockroach through the tunnel streets

from the shanties creaking iron-sheets
violence like a bug-infested rag is tossed
and fear is immanent as sound in the wind-swung bell;

the long day's anger pants from sand and rocks;
but for this breathing night at least,
my land, my love, sleep well.

This Sun on This Rubble

This sun on this rubble after rain.

Bruised though we must be
some easement we require
unarguably, though we argue against desire.

Under jackboots our bones and spirits crunch
forced into sweat-tear-sodden slush
— now glow-lipped by this sudden touch:

— sun-stripped perhaps, our bones may later sing
or spell out some malignant nemesis
Sharpevilled to spearpoints for revenging

but now our pride-dumbed mouths are wide
in wordless supplication
— are grateful for the least relief from pain

— like this sun on this debris after rain.

Poems About Prison

I

Cold

the clammy cement
sucks our naked feet

a rheumy yellow bulb
lights a damp grey wall

the stubbled grass
wet with three o'clock dew
is black with glittery edges;

we sit on the concrete,
stuff with our fingers
the sugarless pap
into our mouths

then labour erect;

form lines;

steel ourselves into fortitude
or accept an image of ourselves
numb with resigned acceptance;

the grizzled senior warder comments:
'Things like these
I have no time for;

they are worse than rats;
you can only shoot them.'

Overhead
the large frosty glitter of the stars
the Southern Cross flowering low;

the chains on our ankles
and wrists
that pair us together
jangle

glitter.

We begin to move
    awkwardly.

(Colesberg: en route to Robben Island)

Mazisi Kunene

The Echoes

Over the vast summer hills
I shall commission the maternal sun
To fetch you with her long tilted rays,

The slow heave of the valleys
Will once again roll the hymns of accompaniment
Scattering the glitter of the milky way over the bare fields.

You will meet me
Underneath the shadow of the timeless earth
Where I lie weaving the seasons.

You will indulge in the sway dances of your kin
To the time of symphonic flutes
Ravishing the identity of water lilies.

I have opened the mountain gates
So that the imposing rim
Of the Ruwenzori shall steal your image.

Even the bubbling lips of continents
(To the shy palms of Libya)
Shall awake the long-forgotten age.

The quivering waters of the Zambezi river
Will bear on a silvery blanket your name
Leading it to the echoing of the sea.

Let me not love you alone
Lest the essence of your being
Lie heavy on my tongue
When you count so many to praise.

Elegy

O Mzingeli son of the illustrious clans
You whose beauty spreads across the Tukela estuary
Your memory haunts like two eagles
We have come to the ceremonial ruins
We come to mourn the bleeding sun
We are the children of Ndungunya of the Dlamini clan
They whose grief strikes fear over the earth
We carry the long mirrors in the afternoon
Recasting time's play past infinite night.

O great departed ancestors
You promised us immortal life with immortal joys
But how you deceived us!

We invited the ugly salamander
To keep watch over a thousand years with a thousand sorrows
She watched to the far end of the sky
Sometimes terrorized by the feet of departed men
One day the furious storms
One day from the dark cyclone
One day in the afternoon
We gazed into a barren desert
Listening to the tremendous voices in the horizon
And loved again in the epics
And loved incestuous love!

We count a million
Strewn in the dust of ruined capitals
The bull tramples us on an anthill
We are late in our birth
Accumulating violent voices
Made from the lion's death
You whose love comes from the stars
Have mercy on us!
Give us the crown of thunder
That our grief may overhang the earth

O we are naked at the great streams
Wanderers greet us no more . . .

Thought on June 26

Was I wrong when I thought
All shall be avenged?
Was I wrong when I thought
The rope of iron holding the neck of young bulls
Shall be avenged?
Was I wrong
When I thought the orphans of sulphur
Shall rise from the ocean?
Was I depraved when I thought there need not be love,
There need not be forgiveness, there need not be progress,
There need not be goodness on the earth,
There need not be towns of skeletons,
Sending messages of elephants to the moon?
Was I wrong to laugh asphyxiated ecstasy
When the sea rose like quicklime
When the ashes on ashes were blown by the wind
When the infant sword was left alone on the hill top?
Was I wrong to erect monuments of blood?
Was I wrong to avenge the pillage of Caesar?
Was I wrong? Was I wrong?
Was I wrong to ignite the earth
And dance above the stars
Watching Europe burn with its civilization of fire,
Watching America disintegrate with its gods of steel,
Watching the persecutors of mankind turn into dust
Was I wrong? Was I wrong?

Sipho Sepamla

On Judgement Day

       black people are born singers
       black people are born runners
       black people are peace-loving
these myths make of us naïvete

we have been sipped with bubbles of champagne
we have known choking dust
and have writhed with the pain of humiliation

       singers
       runners
       peace-loving

nobody really sees the storm raging within us
nobody cares to know that we've reached our own bottom

laughing has become agonizing

       singers
       runners
       peace-loving
            my foot

I fear we will all sing at night-vigils
and as I see things we will all run for cover
what I don't know is which peace will still be lovable

Civilization Aha

i thought of eden
                the first time i ate a fig
i thought of a whiteman
                    the first time I saw god's
                        portrait
i thought of a blackman
                    the first time i met satan on
                        earth
i must be honest
            it wasn't only bantu education
        it was all part of what they say is western
                    civilization

Talk to the Peach Tree

Let's talk to the swallows visiting us in summer
ask how it is in other countries

Let's talk to the afternoon shadow
ask how the day has been so far

Let's raise our pets to our level
ask them what they don't know of us

      words have lost meaning
      like all notations they've been misused

      most people will admit
      a whining woman can overstate her case

Talk to the paralysing heat in the air
inquire how long the mercilessness will last

Let's pick out items from the rubbish heap
ask how the stench is like down there

Let's talk to the peach tree
find out how it feels to be in the ground

Let's talk to the moon going down
ask if it isn't enough eyeing what's been going on

    come on
    let's talk to the devil himself
    it's about time

Don Mattera

Departure

I grow tired
and want to leave this city
seething in unrest and injustice
I am leaving . . .

    No,
    I have already left.

    Look for me
    on the banks of the Nile
    or under some spreading tree.

    I shall be sleeping
    the sleep of freedom
    don't wake me
    leave me to dream
    my dream of departure
    from a city
    seething in unrest,
    void of pity.

    I grow weary of eating brine
    and I hunger for desert fruit . . .

The Poet Must Die . . .

for James Matthews and Gladys Thomas after their poems were executed

The poet must die
His murmuring threatens their survival
His breath could start the revolution;
He must be destroyed.

Ban him.
Send him to the Island
Call the firing-squad.
But remember to wipe his blood
From the wall.
Then destroy the wall
Crush the house
Kill the neighbours.

If their lies are to survive
The poet must die . . .

Sobukwe . . .
on his death

It was our suffering
    and our tears
    that nourished and kept him alive
    their law that killed him.

    Let no dirges be sung
    no shrines be raised
    to burden his memory;
    men such as he
    need no tombstones
    to speak their fame.

Lay him down on a high mountain
that he may look
on the land he loved
the nation he died for

Men feared the fire of his soul . . .

I Have Been Here Before
for my father

When the first sun rose
It found me awake and waiting;
Long before you came to this hill
My footsteps shaped the landscape,
Tamed the buffalo

    I rode the wind,
    Silenced the hurricane

Look at me
I have been here before . . .
    I washed my wounds in the Nile
    Danced in the streets of Egypt
    Slept in the wings of the Scarab,
    Made love to Nefertitti
Look at me
My eyes were stark, black stars
Raging in the night;
Tempests of rebellion
Ancient as life
    Long before the snake
    Came to my children,
    I looked at God's face
    And saw my image in his eyes . . .

Keorapetse Kgositsile

The Air I Hear

The air, I hear,
froze to the sound
searching. And my memory
present and future tickles
the womb like the pulse
of this naked air
in the eye of a tear
drop. The dead cannot
remember even the memory
of death's laughter. But memory
defiant like the sound of pain
rides the wave at dawn
in the marrow of the desert
palm: stands looking still
and the bitter shape
of yesterdays weaves
timeless tomorrows
in the leaves
of laughter larger than
singular birth . . .

Song for Ilva Mackay and Mongane

Hear now a sound of floods
Of desire of longing of memories
Of erstwhile peasants who can
No longer laugh downhill. My brother

Knows there is no death in life
Only in death. That music is native
So I sing your name.

You are child of your tongue
You will be born with gun
In one eye and grenade in the other
You are Tito: There is no such thing
As escape or sanctuary in life where
All things come to pass when they do
Where every bloodstain is a sign of death or life

You are Mandela: You are all
The names we are in Robben Island
You are child of sound and sense
You can look the past
Straight in the eye
To know this season and purpose
You have come from yesterday
To remind the living that
The dead do not remember the banned
The jailed the exiled the dead
Here I meet you
And this way I salute you
With bloodstains on my tongue:

I am no calypsonian
But this you have taught me:
You could say you were from Capetown
Or Johannesburg Accra or Bagamoy
Newyork Kingston or Havana
When you have come from tomorrow
We shall know each other by our bloodstains

The Present is a Dangerous Place to Live

I *In the Mourning*

And at the door of the eye
is the still voice of the land.
My father before my father
knew the uses of fire
My father before my father,
with his multiple godhead,
sat on his circular stool
after the day was done. At times even
between the rednesses of two suns,
knowing that time was not born yesterday.
The circle continues
Time will always be
in spite of minutes that know no life.
Lives change in life
At times even rot
or be trampled underfoot
as the back of a slave.
There are cycles in the circle
I may even moan my deadness
or mourn your death,
in this sterile moment asking:
Where is the life we came to live?
Time will always be
Pastpresentfuture is always now
Where then is the life we came to live?

IV *Mirrors, Without Song*

Do not tell me, my brother, to reach
out and touch my soul. My soul is
inside and thin
and knows your death too

Does it matter then how
often my teeth are seen
when I laugh less and less?

Morning does not wake up
with my eye out the window
moaning, or mourning,
a thing or day gone to waste

I die in the world
and live my deadness
in my head, laughing
less and less.

Do you see now
another day, like a slave,
shows its face to be nothing,
nothing but a mirror of the death of another?

When I laugh, my brother, less and less
do not tell me to reach
out and touch my soul. My
soul is inside and thin
and knows your death too.

When the Deal Goes Down

So now you have become increasingly reticent
It's a long way from the warmth
Of a loving and loved parent
Whose hugs and kisses and mischief

Carry love and care and laughter
Palpable as flowers as a loaf of fresh bread
To this pensive young voice

Papa everything has a reason right

You are stunned to thought
The child is talking dialectics
And you fear what might be coming
You fear what you do not know
Perhaps, you say to the child
But . . . say . . . what are you saying

You know Papa sometimes you come home
Tense and impatient
One little thing we say or do
And you threaten to punish us
You yell at us you tell us
You have had enough of our nonsense

All right do you think there are times
When I have a reason to do that
O-o-o-oh plenty of times
Okay next time when there is no reason
Promise you'll let me know

We dream in our quest
Determined past any argument
To reclaim ourselves our Home
Is the dream thereby insulated
From nightmare which looms and leaps at us
Through the child's anguish
Which has ambushed her laughter

We do not have a mother
Mama is always away
Struggling to liberate us
When she comes home
It is only to sleep

Scientific though you say you are
You feel haunted by uncountable demons
Pounding you amongst the walls of your haggard despair
As the young voice now barbed
And intractable deflates you

I do not know my father
Papa is always busy
He does not know me either
I pick up pieces of my father
From all the uncles I meet
In search of him
Who is my father
I try to fit these pieces together
To give birth to my father
The clear voice that sees you
With the power of collective memory
Slices the core of you and you shudder
As you hear

The vice is getting tighter
And you're standing in between
No place to hide
No place to run

Your whole being is a trapped tangle
And you gasp shuddering again
In the heat of your cold sweat
Reeling and wading through the stench
Of your dream turned juggernaut
And you scream
                    RESCUE ME!
To nobody that you know
To no force you could name
In the moment of when the deal comes down

Montage: Bouctou Lives

Even nature at her best
In singing her mesmerizing beauty
With the permanent rainbow
That is the wonder of Mosioathunya
Says nothing of the woman of Mali

My Mali sisters are a rainbow
Even the deaf and dumb
Would aspire to sing

Here Keats would have found voice
And song instead of the finality
Of deadness
He dubs beauty and love
Though we do not see human gesture
Nor life in his Grecian urn

My sisters of Mali could
        Teach any rainbow
            The impartial beauty
                Of nature through a rainbow
Of centuries of memory and mutations

Look at the flow of that ebony elegance
Walking that walk
Striding through your heart
Turning Bamako into a dream

And that blue-eyed ivory contrast over there
That strut is a vector on the graph
Linking Africa to where
And all of that all in
Between bespeaks where

Which woman have you not met here
In Mali I have seen my mother
My daughter I have seen
My grandmother and her very own too

My wife friends comrades
All the women I love and hurt
All the women without whom
I am not even here
All the women without whom
Neither you nor I
Could claim an identity
Which all that lives has

I wish I had enough
Art of eloquence and grace to sing
The woman of Mali

Oswald Mtshali

Inside My Zulu Hut

It is a hive
without any bees
to build the walls
with golden bricks of honey.
A cave cluttered
with a millstone,
calabashes of sour milk
claypots of foaming beer
sleeping grass mats
wooden head rests
tanned goat skins
tied with riempies
to wattle rafters
blackened by the smoke
of kneaded cow dung
burning under
the three-legged pot
on the earthen floor
to cook my porridge.

Ride upon the Death Chariot

They rode upon
the death chariot
to their Golgotha —

three vagrants
whose papers to be in Caesar's empire
were not in order.

The sun
shrivelled their bodies
in the mobile tomb
as airtight as canned fish.

We're hot!
We're thirsty!
We're hungry!

The centurion
touched their tongues
with the tip
of a lance
dipped in apathy:

'Don't cry to me
but to Caesar who
crucifies you.'

A woman came
to wipe their faces.
She carried a dishcloth
full of bread and tea.

We're dying!

The centurion
washed his hands.

The Birth of Shaka

His baby cry
was of a cub
tearing the neck
of the lioness
because he was fatherless.

The gods
boiled his blood
in a clay pot of passion
to course in his veins.

His heart was shaped into an ox shield
to foil every foe.

Ancestors forged
his muscles into
thongs as tough
as wattle bark
and nerves
as sharp as
syringa thorns.

His eyes were lanterns
that shone from the dark valleys of Zululand
to see white swallows
coming across the sea.
His cry to two assassin brothers:

'Lo! you can kill me
but you'll never rule this land!'

Arthur Nortje

Up Late

Night here, the owners asleep upstairs:
the room's eyes shut, its voices dead,
though I admire it when its mirrors
oblige me with my presence. Looking ahead
needs glancing back to what I once
was, the time that mischance
borrowed my body to break it by terror.

Now the cameras rest in their elegant
leather coffins, having caught
the whirl of streets before the wheels go silent.
Rain trickles as the red biro writes my heart:
time demands no attention of the will,
the clock is yellow with black numerals.
The icebox resumes its purring descant.

This picture opens on the past. I rise
to study a calendar scene from what was home:
an old white mill, sentimental, South African Airways
(the blue lithe buck), peaceful, implausible. Some
fugitive sense holds back the bruising wave:
that gift to spend, my song where I arrive,
didn't I take it from the first dispiriting wilderness?

My mind burned and I shackled it
with squalid love, the violence of the flesh.
The quiet scars over my veins bit
less deep now than the knife or lash
could feel content about:

no longer need I shout
freedom in the house. I sit in light

here, the refugee's privilege. Nor do I want
fruit in a bowl, banana pleasure, the skin
that slides from my fingers, spent
because the soft heart only must be eaten.
Give me the whole experience to savour
who have known waste and also favour:
time to come may find me eloquent

in other rooms, that reminisce
of this one so composed in silence. Love,
the necessary pain, has spurred a search.
Moving from place to place I always have
come some way closer to knowing
the final sequence of song that's going
to master the solitudes night can teach.

At Rest from the Grim Place

The sergeant laughs with strong teeth,
his jackboots nestle under the springbok horns.
Those bayonets are silent,
the spear of the nation gone to the ground.
Warriors prowl in the stars of their dungeons.
I've seen the nebulae of a man's eyes
squirm with pain, he sang his life
through cosmic volleys. They call it
genital therapy, the blond bosses.

Why is there no more news?
Bluetits scuffle in the eaves of England,
an easy summer shimmers on the water.
Fields of peace, I lie here
in the music of your gaze
so beautiful we seem no strangers.

Curling smoke, a white butt is
brother to my lips and fingers.
You watch the ash on grass blades gently crumble.
Your hands are small as roses,
they cancel memory.

Once going down to the sea through the mountains
my limbs felt freedom in the glide of air:
over the bridge at the window I found
speech an impossible cry.
Under the fatal shadows spun down the chasm
my heart squirmed in the throat of snaking water.
I have since forgotten what they call that place.

Mongane Wally Serote

The Growing

No!
This is not dying when the trees
Leave their twigs
To grow blindly long into windows like fingers into eyes.
And leave us unable
To wink or to blink or to actually close the eye,
The mind –
Twigs thrusting into windows and leaves falling on the sills,
Are like thoughts uncontrolled and stuffing the heart.
Yes,
This is teaching about the growing of things:
If you crowd me I'll retreat from you,
If you still crowd me I'll think a bit,
Not about crowding you but about your right to crowd me;
If you still crowd me, I will not, but I will be thinking
About crowding you.
If my thoughts and hands reach out
To prune the twigs and sweep the leaves,
There was a growth of thought here,
Then words, then action.
So if I say prune instead of cut,
I'm teaching about the growing of things.

Hell, Well, Heaven

I do not know where I have been,
But Brother,
I know I'm coming.
I do not know where I have been,
But Brother,
I know I heard the call,
Hell! where I was I cried silently
Yet I sat there until now.
I do not know where I have been,
But Brother,
I know I'm coming:
I come like a tide of water now,
But Oh! there's sand beneath me!
I do not know where I have been
To feel so weak, Heavens! so weary.
But Brother,
Was that Mankunku's* horn?
Hell! my soul aches like a body that has been beaten,
Yet I endured till now.
I do not know where I have been,
But Brother,
I know I'm coming.
I do not know where I have been,
But Brother I come like a storm over the veld,
And Oh! there are stone walls before me!
I do not know where I have been
To have fear so strong like the whirlwind (will it be that brief?)
But Brother,
I know I'm coming.
I do not know where I have been,
But Brother,
Was that Dumile's† figure?

* Mankunku: a musician.
† Dumile: a sculptor.

Hell, my mind throbs like a heart beat, there's no peace;
And my body of wounds – when will they be scars? –
Yet I can still walk and work and still smile.
I do not know where I have been
But Brother,
I know I'm coming.
I do not know where I have been,
But Brother,
I have a voice like the lightning-thunder over the mountains.
But Oh! there are copper lightning conductors for me!
I do not know where I have been
To have despair so deep and deep and deep
But Brother,
I know I'm coming.
I do not know where I have been
But Brother.
Was that Thoko's* voice?
Hell, well, Heavens!

Ofay-Watcher Looks Back

I want to look at what happened;
That done,
As silent as the roots of plants pierce the soil
I look at what happened,
Whether above the houses there is always either smoke or dust,
As there are always flies above a dead dog.
I want to look at what happened.
That done,
As silent as plants show colour: green,
I look at what happened,
When houses make me ask: do people live there?
As there is something wrong when I ask – is that man alive?
I want to look at what happened.

* Thoko: a singer.

That done,
As silent as the life of a plant that makes you see it
I look at what happened
When knives creep in and out of people
As day and night into time.
I want to look at what happened,
That done,
As silent as plants bloom and the eye tells you:
                        something has happened.
I look at what happened.
When jails are becoming necessary homes for people
Like death comes out of disease,

I want to look at what happened.

From *Come and Hope with Me* (1995)

In that day and in that life
we lived in dreams and also in desire
we hoped and believed
even when the day crushed and popped our time
turning the sky crimson and the night cast upon us
dark and cold shadows
and the sky, stern, hovered above us
we lived in dreams and hopes

strong
we sang
we chanted
we jumped and danced
and we were aware of the steep and slope of the road
and of the load on our shoulders.
with skill
we lived in dreams and desire
loving life with our large hearts
even though nostalgia like fire
burnt and burnt our gut

all these
we mounted, jumped and chanted
our eyes fixed on the road

remember
the passion of our hearts
the blinding ache and pain
when we heard the hysterical sobs
of our little children crying against fate
which violated them and offered them no life
or the frightening cry of a man
who climbs life with no hope in his heart
we heard these. we knew them. we absorbed them
but we surged forward
knowing that life is a promise and that that promise is us
the promise lives in the staring eye of a song

Gcina Mhlophe

Sometimes When It Rains

Sometimes when it rains
I smile to myself
And think of times when as a child
I'd sit by myself
And wonder why people need clothes

Sometimes when it rains
I think of times
when I'd run into the rain
Shouting 'Nkce – nkce mlanjana
When will I grow?
I'll grow up tomorrow!'

Sometimes when it rains
I think of times
When I watched goats
running so fast from the rain
While sheep seemed to enjoy it

Sometimes when it rains
I think of times
When we had to undress
Carry the small bundles of uniforms and books
On our heads
And cross the river after school

Sometimes when it rains
I remember times
When it would rain hard for hours
And fill our drum

so we didn't have to fetch water
From the river for a day or two

Sometimes when it rains
Rains for many hours without break
I think of people
who have nowhere to go
No home of their own
And no food to eat
Only rain water to drink

Sometimes when it rains
Rains for days without break
I think of mothers
Who give birth in squatter camps
Under plastic shelters
At the mercy of cold angry winds

Sometimes when it rains
I think of 'illegal' job seekers
in big cities
Dodging police vans in the rain
Hoping for darkness to come
So they can find some wet corner to hide in

Sometimes when it rains
Rains so hard hail joins in
I think of life prisoners
in all the jails of the world
And wonder if they still love
To see the rainbow at the end of the rain

Sometimes when it rains
With hail stones biting the grass
I can't help thinking they look like teeth
Many teeth of smiling friends
Then I wish that everyone else
Had something to smile about.

Uganda

Okot p'Bitek

From *The Song of Lawino* (1966)

Listen, my clansmen,
I cry over my husband
Whose head is lost.
Ocol has lost his head
In the forest of books.

When my husband
Was still wooing me
His eyes were still alive,
His ears were still unblocked,
Ocol had not yet become a fool
My friend was a man then!

He had not yet become a woman,
He was still a free man,
His heart was still his chief.

My husband was still a Black man
The son of the Bull
The son of Agik
The woman from Okol
Was still a man,
An Acoli . . .

The papers on my husband's desk
Coil threateningly
Like the giant forest climbers,
Like the kituba tree
That squeezes other trees to death;
Some stand up,
Others lie on their backs,

They are interlocked
Like the legs of youths
At the orak dance,
Like the legs of the planks
Of the goggo fence,
They are tightly interlocked
Like the legs of the giant forest climbers
In the impenetrable forest.

My husband's house
Is a mighty forest of books,
Dark it is and very damp,
The steam rising from the ground
Hot thick and poisonous
Mingles with the corrosive dew
And the rain drops
That have collected in the leaves . . .

Oh, my clansmen,
Let us all cry together!
Come,
Let us mourn the death of my husband,
The death of a Prince
The Ash that was produced
By a great Fire!
O, this homestead is utterly dead,
Close the gates
With lacari thorns,
For the Prince
The heir to the Stool is lost!
And all the young men
Have perished in the wilderness!
And the fame of this homestead
That once blazed like wild fire
In a moonless night
Is now like the last breaths
Of a dying old man!

There is not one single true son left,
The entire village
Has fallen into the hands
Of war captives and slaves!
Perhaps one of our boys
Escaped with his life!
Perhaps he is hiding in the bush
Waiting for the sun to set!

But will he come?
Before the next mourning?
Will he arrive in time?

Bile burns my inside!
I feel like vomiting!
For all our young men
Were finished in the forest,
Their manhood was finished
In the class-rooms,
Their testicles
Were smashed
With large books!

From *Song of Prisoner* (1970)

Is today not my father's
Funeral anniversary?

My clansmen and clanswomen
Are gathering in our village,
They sit in circles
In the shades of granaries,
But who will make
The welcome speech?

Men drink kwete beer,
Women cook goat meat
And make millet bread,

But I am not there
To distribute the dishes
Among the elders!
The priests throw morsels
Of chicken meat,
They squirt goat blood
And pour libations
To the assembled ghosts
Of the dead,
But how can I address
The ghosts of my fathers
From here?
How can they put chymes
On my chest and back?
How can my grandmother
Spit blessing on me?

My age-mates have donned
White ostrich feathers,
They are singing a war song,
I want to join them
In the wilderness
And chase Death away
From our village,
Drive him a thousand miles
Beyond the mountains
In the west,
Let him sink down
With the setting sun
And never rise again.

I want to join
The funeral dancers,
I want to tread the earth
With a vengeance
And shake the bones
Of my father in his grave!

Richard Ntiru

If It is True

If it is true
that the world talks too much
then let's all keep quiet
and hear the eloquence
of silence

If it is true
that the world sees too much
then let's all close our eyes
and see the inner vision
beneath the closed eyes

If it is true
that the world hears too much
then let's wax our ears
and listen to the chastity of inner music
that defies betrayal
by the wayward wind

If it is true
that the world moves too much
then let's stand statuestill
and imitate the stubborn will
of trees
that move without being peripatetic

for the dumb don't tell lies

for the blind can't be peeping-toms

for the deaf cannot eavesdrop

for the crippled can't trespass.

The Miniskirt

To visualize what you can't see;
That's the paradoxical pleasure of the mind.

In the afterbirth of seeing,
Death of imagination.

To dally on the brink of reality:
That's the snug illusion of life.

In the capitulation of the summit,
Paradoxical disappointment.

Now is the legend beyond
Become the cliché of the elements.

Shall the synthetic gauze
Atone for the beauty of the fertility lines?

Zambia

Gwendoline Konie

In the Fist of Your Hatred

Like a worm I writhe in your tight fist
As you try to smother my voice
And my mind with your brutal grip;
Fear stalks the house of my brain
As your pepper-red eyes shout blood.

Your grip strangles my tongue
Your fingers sprinkle seeds of fear in my mind
And it sprouts like a raging bush fire.
You have set up fear as my companion
And I cringe from your bloodshot eyes.

Secret alarm bells sear my brain
And leave me burning with a wild rage
For I will not let fear swallow
My breath, my dreams, and my hopes!
My hidden courage will saw off your fist.

Zimbabwe

Hopewell Seyaseya

The Hereafter

The serenity of the graves, the air,
The stones, the engraved names and dates;
The stillness of the cemented atmosphere
Imprison the dead in the forest of death.
Is flesh and blood the source of distress
And joy? To be burnt without a yell
Or rejoice without a sound
Is for the tacit skulls underneath to explain.
And there I long to retire for the burden
Is heavy even for atlas,
And no simons of Africa will take the load off me.
My brother's unmarked grave
Only takes me to a dream and I get no closer to him
Than in my first death, and homeward I turn
To the whims of life and the certain death of man.
As the night closes in on my first life, and
My flesh and blood forewarns me of the impending
Day of revelation, through the chambers
Of my undoubting mind, I behold a graceful run
Of brotherly spirits, an everlasting embrace and
A perpetual joy of souls awaiting me in the hereafter.

Nightsong

Silvery in the moonlight night
The river of my mind flows
To the nightsong of the truly great
Entombed in the caves of history
At heroes' acre. The music
Crescending through the valley
Of ghost towns and stabbed villages
Will come down to settle on our hearts
Like dew on leaves, tears for those
Who surrendered their lives at the altar
Leaving in us an eternal flame.

Albert Chimedza

I screw my brother's wife

I screw my brother's wife
I am the slithering snake in the grass
I am the yukky stuff that clogs the veins of the government
I am the leech that sucks the national purse.

Look at my two tone shoes from Milan
Real tweed suit from London – Prince Charles wears one like it
Metal facility Walkman from L.A.
Best vodka in town from my last trip to Moscow
I am the maggot that feeds off a juicy beast called ZIMCORD.

You must admit my video is good
I got it duty free in Brussels
I even managed a video copy of 'Deep Throat' with the change
Now I can watch 'Dallas' in colour
I have an eye for a good buy.

I am a little fella called the bottomless pit
I am a good citizen, I have faith in the government.
I never tire of gorging the good life
I have friends in the right places
I shall buy my personal copy of 'Staying Alive'
On my conference trip to Paris next week.

Now that my mind flies

Now that my mind flies
With the power of the wings of a gull
Now that the sea
Has taken on a most disconsolate air
And now that the harsh winds
Of a storm from some place unknown
Speak out in anguish and tremble
The soft grass in its seaside bed
Now that you are standing next to me
Grafted in my mind
At this cliff's edge where all around me
Is whispering death death death.

You are not here and the dreaded moment has come
I the accused am the judge
The assembled jury has taken on a most solemn air
What is there left but to turn around and run
Thereby cheating death yet another time?

Now that there is reticence
That freezes the warm rays of the retiring sun
Now that you will stay and I will go
I fighting to forget and you to remember
How can I look you in the eye and brace myself to say;
Now is the day the moment and the place
Take your pieces of gold and run?

Dambudzo Marechera

Answer to a Complaint

How long should your holler
Redeem the arthritis in the street?
Your life's contract mentions no
Assurances about meaning or fulfilment.

Indeed our list says you do not exist
Therefore these despairs about the Bomb
Do not exist. We announce in the next report
How people like you are exactly going to be dealt with.

In fact measures are already in train
To railroad your destructive human tendencies;
Drink your regulation tea with a spoon of caution.
Your fears exist only on the paper of which flesh is made.

Punkpoem

In the song
Are waterfruits;
In the plush and flow
Firestars eternally fixed.

Guitar strings lash
My back, draw blood –
The out-of-control voice
Skids shrieking across

Tarmac audiences.

The Bar-stool Edible Worm

I am against everything
Against war and those against
War. Against whatever diminishes
Th'individual's blind impulse.

Shake the peaches down from
The summer poem, Rake in ripe
Luminosity; dust; taste. Lunchtime
News – pass the Castor Oil, Alice.

Dido in Despair

No broom can sweep away the dust
Of your departure. Night's granules
Like a swarm of locusts, have driven out
The Arabian carpet, that enchanted time,
Leaving me buffeted by hailstorms of doubt
And despair.

Black sunlight, granitic water
Flames encased in sheets of ice,
My heart can only read in the dark,
My footsteps are planted firmly on empty air,
My eyes, seeking answers, peer backward into my brains.

Musaemura Bonas Zimunya

Tarantula

Such is your fate tarantula
for emerging red-claw raised between my pillows
so early in the morning to ambush my nerves
I lost my decision awhile as the space
I knew so well diminished in the search
for weapons – books, combs, and chairs.

Your hands and legs – pedipalps – bend to your face
with the pain of the spray-bursts held so long
like a fire extinguisher. How are you dead
when my ankles and my hind-arm
still echo my fears with aching burning?

Such repose, Arachnida, your unsuspecting fate
for tenderly – stealthily – endlessly searching
for prey and resting nooks in human surroundings.

Your long, hairy legs interlock
finally, stiff.

See Through

My heart here
rages with sun-presence
and the noisy open street
to embrace indian soft
female limbs

whose coppery warmth
defies garments and
hosiery

My desire is stayed
because I am left
abandoned in the growl
of traffic as the moment
leapt out of my hands.

I am seen
naked in my eyes.

Her

Her kisses left my lips
stinging like a shaven chin

her bed-grip left my back
aching with vice-pain

and breathing she snuffed me out
like a birthday candle

but I make no plea to the gods
as she was my portal and my baptism

Jikinya
(An African Passion)

While metals roar and flame
heads and feet smell of burning
men enthuse about commanding Death
and a sad wind ululates across the raped land

Dance, Jikinya, dance

Eyes of you surprised round-nuts
as for a moment the rainbow around your head vanishes
into mist surrounding pedalling limbs
trembling belly and bosom in rising smoke
as you dance to the rhythm of thunder
and gorge howling at the Zambezi water

as stars hawk-eyed and vulture-beaked
tear the drums with unrelenting frenzy
the restless song bubbles in tears
and life bleeds all over the land

Dance, Jikinya, dance
as the figures of fate
battle roll, scramble and roar
with the tones of Babel
in a frantic search for the exit

Tamba Jikinya naBaba

though your knees cut
your breath stabs
your feet are blistered
your back peels
and your face is a mirror of horrified shadows

Kristina Rungano

After the Rain

The spots triumphed in the afternoon light;
There where the sun had at some time forgotten its duty
And somewhere higher up
The leaves bristled in the breeze
Devoid of shame they shook their bodies
And there where butterflies had perished
The soft raindrops had found a home
And about places where friend and foe had roamed
A gentle light seeped thro' from the white sky
And there the sorcerer's hand
From when it touched the flakes of water, they glistened
Till from afar they looked like virgin clouds
And one could almost feel their twinkle.

Yet no one dared look into the heavens
Nor learn that this was a time of silence
No bird, nor insect; grasshopper, mosquito, fly
Dared venture there where lightning had left its mark
Flocks of humanity had begun to fly from the roadsides
And for the moment serenity had captured its whoring wards
For whom peace would never be complete
And when finally the sun found courage
One was surprised to find that evening had so prematurely
    descended
And it was too late to disturb the solitude which crept in
Tomorrow the trees'd look a day more ancient
Yet still it would be
The same familiar beautiful Zimbabwe.

Notes on the Authors

Aidoo, Ama Ata: b. 1942 at Abeadzi Kyiakor, Central Ghana; graduated in English at Legon; has worked as university lecturer at Cape Coast and as Minister of Education. She has published plays, novels, stories and poems over thirty years, starting with her celebrated play *Dilemma of a Ghost* in 1965. Now lives in Zambia.

Aig-Imoukhuede, Frank: b. 1935 at Elunabon, near Ile-Ife, Nigeria. Attended Igbobi College, and University College Ibadan, where he contributed to J. P. Clark's poetry magazine, *The Horn*. Has spent most of his career in information. One of the few poets since Adelaide Casely-Hayford to write poetry in Pidgin.

Aiyejina, Funso: b. 1949 in Edo State, Western Nigeria; studied at universities of Ife, Acadia (Canada) and the West Indies. Taught for ten years at Ife University and now lives in Trinidad. His first volume, *A Letter to Lynda and Other Poems* (Saros), won the Poetry Prize from the Association of Nigerian Authors in 1988. A new volume, *Of Generals and Kings, Priests and Poets*, is forthcoming from Saros. One of Nigeria's finest satirists, his poems have often appeared in *West Africa* and other journals.

Amadiume, Ifi: b. near Enugu in Eastern Nigeria; now lives and works in London. First collection, *Passion Waves*, published in London by Karnak Press in 1986.

Andrade, Costa: b. 1936 at Huambo, Angola. Studied architecture in Lisbon and Yugoslavia and was a leading figure in the Case dos Estudantes do Império. Served with MPLA guerrillas from 1968 to 1974. Has published poetry, short stories and criticism, including: *Terra de acácias rubras* (Lisbon, 1961); *Tempo Angolan em Italia* (São Paolo, 1963); *O Regresso e o Canto* (Lobito, 1975); *Poesia com Armas* (Lisbon, 1975); *O Caderno dos Heróis* (Luanda, 1977).

Anyidoho, Kofi: b. 1947 at Wheta, Ghana. Trained as a teacher before entering University of Ghana to read English and Linguistics. Whilst in the

USA for higher studies published *Elegy for the Revolution* (1980). His poetry has also appeared in *Okike, Ch'indaba* and *West Africa*. Further collections include *A Harvest of Our Dreams* (Heinemann, 1984) and *Earthchild* (Accra, Woeli Publications, 1985). Now teaches in Ghana.

Armah, Ayi Kwei: b. 1939 in Takoradi, southern Ghana; studied at Achimota and Harvard. Best known as one of Africa's most powerful and original novelists ever since the publication of *The Beautiful Ones Are Not Yet Born* in 1968. Armah has lived and worked in many African countries, including Algeria, Tanzania and Botswana, as well as Ghana.

Asalache, Khadambi: b. 1934 at Kaimosi, Kenya. Studied art and architecture in Nairobi and Vienna, then worked in London for several years. Has published a novel, *A Calabash of Life* (Longman, 1967).

Awoonor, Kofi: b. 1935 at Wheta, Ghana. Studied at Achimota, University of Ghana, London and New York. Edited the literary review *Okyeame* in the early sixties. After the fall of Kwame Nkrumah, spent some ten years in Britain and the USA before returning to Ghana in 1976 and joining University of Cape Coast. Has published *Rediscovery* (Ibadan, Mbari, 1964); *Night of My Blood* (Doubleday, 1971); *Ride Me, Memory* (Greenfield Review Press, 1973); *The House by the Sea* (Greenfield Review Press, 1978); a study of Ewe traditional poetry, *Guardians of the Sacred Word* (Nok Publications, 1974); a novel, *This Earth, My Brother* (Doubleday, 1971); and a study of African traditional culture, *The Breast of the Earth* (Doubleday, 1972). Awonoor was imprisoned for a year in Usher's Fort (The House by the Sea) just before Jerry Rawlings came to power. Since then he has served as ambassador in Brazil and Cuba. His collected poems, *Until the Morning After*, were published by Greenfield Review Press in 1987.

Ba, Oumar: b. 1900 in Mauritania; has published many studies and translations of Peul poetry, including *Poèmes peuls modernes*. His French poetry was collected in *Paroles plaisantes au coeur et à l'oreille* (la Pensée Universelle, 1977).

Barolong, Seboni: b. in Botswana, spent some of his childhood in London and later studied and taught in the USA. He returned to Botswana in 1983 and is now Senior Lecturer in English at the university. He is co-founder of the University of Botswana's Writers' Workshop and has published several volumes of poetry, including *Images of the Sun* and *Thinking Allowed*.

Bognini, Joseph Miezan: b. 1936 at Grand Bassam, Côte d'Ivoire. Studied architecture in Paris. Published his poetry in *Ce dur appel de l'espoir* (Présence Africaine, 1960) and *Herbe féconde* (P. J. Oswald, 1973), as well as many individual poems in *Présence Africaine*.

Bolamba, Antoine-Roger: b. 1913 in Congo-Kinshasa. Published many poems and articles in the journal *La Voix du congolais*, which he edited. Published *Esanzo* (Présence Africaine, 1956).

Brew, Kwesi: b. 1928 at Cape Coast, Ghana. Studied at University of Ghana and worked for many years as a diplomat. Published his poetry in *Shadows of Laughter* (Longman, 1968) and in *Okyeame*.

Brutus, Dennis: b. 1924 in Zimbabwe. Taught for many years in South Africa and campaigned against racism in sport, being himself a keen sportsman. Shot in Johannesburg by South African police and jailed for eighteen months. After leaving Robben Island he was 'banned' and went to London in 1966. Now a Professor at North-Western University, Chicago. Many of his volumes of poetry were collected in *A Simple Lust* (Heinemann, 1973).

Cheney-Coker, Syl: b. 1945 in Freetown, Sierra Leone. Studied there and in the USA. Has been a drummer, journalist and radio producer, before turning to teaching. Moved to University of Maiduguri, Nigeria, in 1978. Has published three volumes of poetry, *Concert for an Exile* (Heinemann, 1973) and *The Graveyard Also Has Teeth* (Heinemann, 1980); a third volume, *The Blood in the Desert's Eyes*, was published in 1990, along with an epic first novel, *The Last Harmattan of Alisoune Dunbar*. Cheney-Coker now edits a newspaper in Freetown.

Chimedza, Albert: b. in Zimbabwe, he published his first collection, *Counterpoint*, jointly with Hopewell Seyaseya in 1984.

Chimombo, Steve: b. 1945 in Zomba, Malawi, where he is now Professor of English. Apart from his activities as dramatist and poet, Chimombo is also editor and proprietor of a literary magazine. *Napolo and the Python*, published by Heinemann in 1994, joined two earlier volumes of poetry with some new pieces.

Chipasula, Frank: b. 1949 of Malawian–Zambian parentage, he studied at Zambia, Brown and Yale universities. Has taught in USA for many years, choosing exile during the long dictatorship of Hastings Banda, the subject of much of his verse. Has published poetry in many journals, as well as two principal collections, *O Earth, Wait For Me* (Johannesburg, Ravan Press, 1984) and *Whispers in the Wings* (Heinemann, 1991). His first novel, *In a Dark Season*, was also published by Heinemann. Joint editor, with his wife, Stella Chipasula, of *African Women's Poetry*.

Chipasula, Stella: b. in Malawi and studied at Providence Teachers' College. After several years teaching, she moved to America and graduated in Art History from the University of Nebraska, where she works in the Library. Edited *African Women's Poetry* jointly with Frank Chipasula.

Clark, John Pepper: b. 1935 in the Delta area of Nigeria. Studied at Government College, Ughelli, and University College, Ibadan, where he founded the poetry magazine *The Horn* in the 1950s. Taught for many years at Lagos University. Well known as a poet, dramatist, critic and translator. Many of his earlier poems were collected in *A Decade of Tongues* (Longman, 1981). His translation of the Ijaw classic, *The Ozidi Saga*, is a major contribution to the study of African oral literature. His collection *State of the Union* was published by Longman in 1985.

Craveirinha, José: b. 1922 at Lourenzo Marques (now Maputo), Mozambique. Worked for many years as a journalist before joining FRELIMO. His poetry has appeared in many journals and anthologies, including Andrade's.

d'Erneville, Annette M'Baye: b. 1927 in Sokhone. An active broadcaster, editor and publisher, she was founder of *Awa: Revue de la femme noire*. Her collection *Kadda* was published in Dakar by the Imprimerie Diop in 1966.

de Sousa, Noémia: b. 1927 at Lourenzo Marques (now Maputo), Mozambique. Very active in the liberation struggle in its early years, she later left Mozambique and lived quietly in exile. Her poetry has been widely published in literary journals and anthologies, including Andrade's.

Diop, Birago: b. 1906 at Dakar, Senegal. Studied at Lycée Faidherbe in St Louis and later qualified as a veterinary surgeon. Spent much of his life in Upper Volta as a government veterinary officer. His output was small, but carefully and exquisitely composed. Had several poems in Senghor's anthology. Published *Leurres et lueurs* (Présence Africaine, 1960), *Les Contes d'Amadou Koumba* (Fasquelle, 1947), *Les Nouveaux Contes d'Amadou Koumba* (Présence Africaine, 1958). The last two volumes are French versions of the folk-tales of a famous storyteller. Birago Diop died in 1989.

Diop, David: b. 1927 at Bordeaux of a Senegalese father and a Cameroonian mother. Killed in an air-crash off Dakar in 1960. Throughout his short life Diop was in poor health and was often in hospital. Moved frequently from his childhood onwards between France and West Africa. Was a regular contributor to *Présence Africaine* and had several early poems in Senghor's anthology. Published *Coups de pilon*, poems (Présence Africaine, 1956).

Dipoko, Mbella Sonne: b. 1936 at Mungo, Cameroon. Educated in West Cameroon and Nigeria. Left for Paris in 1960 and has lived there ever since, devoting himself mainly to poetry and painting. Has published two novels, *A Few Nights and Days* (Longman, 1966) and *Because of Women* (Heinemann, 1974). Was a frequent contributor to *Transition* and *Présence Africaine*. Published his poetry in *Black and White in Love* (Heinemann, 1972).

Dongala, Emmanuel: b. 1941 in Congo Republic. Has published poems in several journals and a novel, *Un fusil dans la main, un poème dans la poche* (Albin Michel, 1973).

Echeruo, Michael: b. 1937 in Eastern Nigeria and educated at University College, Ibadan. Has held many senior academic posts in Nigeria. Published his first collection, *Mortality*, with Longman in 1968.

Fatoba, Femi: b. 1939 in Western Nigeria; studied at Central School of Speech and Drama in London and at University of Minnesota. Fatoba is noted as actor, dancer, drummer, painter and director, as well as poet and dramatist. He has directed many exciting productions whilst teaching Theatre Arts at Ibadan. His first collection of poems, *Petals of Thought*, was published by New Beacon Books in London in 1984.

Higo, Aig: b. 1942 in Mid-Western Nigeria. Studied at Ibadan University. After some years teaching, joined Heinemann and rose to become Managing Director of the Nigerian branch. Contributed frequently to *Transition* and *Black Orpheus*.

Jacinto, Antonio: b. 1924 in Luanda, Angola. Was a pioneer in the movement of cultural nationalism which preceded the armed struggle. Sentenced to fourteen years' imprisonment for being an MPLA militant. Escaped from Portugal in 1973 to join ranks of MPLA and served in government from 1975 onwards. Published *Poemas* (Lisbon, 1961).

Jemie, Onwuchekwa: b. 1941 at Item in Imo State, Nigeria. Studied at Columbia and Harvard universities in the USA. Taught at both Columbia and Minnesota before returning to Nigeria. Currently working as a journalist in Lagos. His first book of poems, *Voyage*, was published by Papua Pocket Poets in 1971 and he has frequently appeared in *Okike*. Is co-author of *Towards the Decolonization of African Literature* (Enugu, 1980).

Johnson, Lemuel: b. in Maiduguri, Northern Nigeria, of Sierra Leonean parents, Johnson was educated in Freetown, France and the USA. He has published the poetic trilogy *Highlife for Caliban*, *Hand on the Navel* and *Carnival for the Old Coast*. His poetry is learned and witty, with a wide range of historical, literary and geographical allusions to establish, as he says, 'a strategic deployment of contexts in my Sierra Leone Krio heritage'. He is at present Professor of English at the University of Michigan, Ann Arbor.

Kadima-Nzuji, Mukula: b. 1947 at Lubumbashi, Congo-Kinshasa. Member of a family prominent in literature and affairs. Has published *Les Ressacs* (Kinshasa, 1969), *Préludes à la terre* (Kinshasa, 1971), and *Redire les mots anciens* (Paris, 1977).

Kalimbakatha, Albert: b. 1967 at Ntcheu, Malawi, where he teaches in the Distance Education Centre. Several of his poems have been broadcast and published locally.

Kane, Amadou Elimane: b. of Fulani stock at Dagana in Senegal. His first collection, *Les Rayons de la Calebasse*, was published by Editions Nouvelles du Sud in 1995. It displays a lyrical talent for weaving together his wide circles of family, friends and lovers with the equally wide landscapes of the Fouta Toro.

Kariara, Jonathan: b. 1935 in Kikuyuland, Kenya. Educated at Makerere University, where he began publishing many poems and short stories. Has worked for many years with publishers in Nairobi and contributes regularly to *Zuka*.

Kayo, Patrice: b. 1942 in the Bamileke country of N.W. Cameroon. Many of his poems have appeared in *Présence Africaine*. Has published *Hymnes et sagesses* (Paris, 1970); *Paroles intimes* (Paris, 1972); and *Chansons populaires Bamilekés* (Yaoundé, n.d.).

Kgositsile, Keorapetse: b. 1938 in Johannesburg, South Africa. Has lived for many years in the USA and published most of his work there, apart from several poems in *Okike* and *Transition*. He was a pioneer of the more angry and abrupt style which later appeared in the work of Serote, Sepamla and others. *To the Bitter End* was published by Third World Press, Chicago, in 1995.

Komey, Ellis Ayitey: b.1927 in Accra, Ghana, where he attended Accra Academy. Sometime editor of *Flamingo* magazine and a contributor to *Black Orpheus* and *West African Review*.

Konie, Gwendoline: b. in Zambia, she was formerly Zambian ambassador to the United Nations. Now a businesswoman in Lusaka, where she edits *Women's Exclusive*.

Kunene, Mazisi: b.1932 in Durban, South Africa, where he took an MA. Came to England in 1959 and worked for the African National Congress whilst continuing his study of Zulu poetry. His own work is usually composed in Zulu and then translated into English by the poet himself. Since the mid seventies he has been a Professor of African Literature at the University of California, Los Angeles. His books include *Zulu Poems* (Deutsch, 1970), *Emperor Shaka the Zulu* (London, 1979) and *Anthem of the Decades* (London, 1981).

Laing, Kojo: b.1946 in Kumasi, Ghana; studied in Ghana and at Glasgow University. Best known as a novelist, he published his first novel, *Search, Sweet Country*, in 1986 and his first volume of poetry, *Godhorse*, in 1989, both with Heinemann. Has held various administrative posts in Ghana, including Secretary of the Institute of African Studies at Legon.

Makisosila, Mawete: b.1955 in Angola, where his father was active in the revolt against Portuguese rule from 1961 onwards. Spent several years in exile in Congo-Kinshasa before returning to Angola to join the MPLA. *Chants polyphoniques des pogroms de Luanda* published jointly with Massaki in 1995.

Malangatana, Valente Ngwenya: b.1936 at Marracuene, Mozambique, and began drawing at an early age. His mother went mad when he was a child and his father was usually away at the mines in South Africa. After joining the studio of the architect Amancio Guedes he developed as a painter of great power and originality. His poems appeared in *Black Orpheus* during the sixties.

Mapanje, Jack: b. 1944 at Kadango, southern Malawi. Studied at Malawi and London universities and became a Lecturer at Chancellor College, Zomba. A founder and editor of *ODI*, a journal of Malawi literature (founded 1971), and a contributor to *MAU: 39 Poems from Malawi* (Blantyre, 1971). First collection, *Of Chameleons and Gods*, published by Heinemann in 1981. Upon republication of his first collection, Mapanje was arrested and held in Mikuyu Jail for three and a half years, without charge or trial. Released suddenly in 1991, he moved to England and published the poems of his prison years in *The Chattering Magpies of Mikuyu Prison* (1993). Other publications also include *Oral Poetry from Africa* (Longman, 1983) and *Summer Fires* (Heinemann, 1983).

Marechera, Dambudzo: b. 1955 in Zimbabwe, Marechera was expelled from the then University of Rhodesia as an activist and spent a year at New College, Oxford. His collection of angry, painful stories, *The House of Hunger* (1978), won him instant recognition and the *Guardian* Fiction Prize. He followed it with his one novel, *Black Sunlight*, in 1980. Upon return to Harare, Marechera led a rough and Bohemian existence. He died suddenly in Harare in 1987. His poetry was published posthumously in *Cemetery of the Mind* (Baobab Books, Harare) in 1992.

Massaki, Makuzayi: b. 1950 in Angola, where his father worked as a journalist and founded an early nationalist party, the PDA. Moving into exile, Massaki spent several years teaching Angola refugee children in Kinshasa, before joining the military wing of the FNLA in 1974. Joint author with Makisosila of *Chants polyphoniques des pogroms de Luanda* (1995).

Mattera, Don: b. 1935 in Western Native Township, South Africa, Mattera played football for Sophiatown, led a street gang, joined the Muslim faith and founded a black journalists' union. Many of his poems appeared in *Staffrider* and the *Star*. His first collection, *Azanian Love Song*, was published by Skotaville, Johannesburg, in 1983. His memoir of Sophiatown, *Gone with the Twilight*, was published in 1987.

Maunick, Edouard: b. 1931 at Port Louis, Mauritius, where he published his first volume, *Ces oiseaux de sang*, before leaving for Paris, where he worked for several years with *Présence Africaine*. His major collection, *Les Manèges de la mer*, was published by Présence Africaine in 1964.

Mnthali, Felix: b. 1933 in northern Malawi. Studied at Malawi and Cambridge universities. Visited Ibadan University, Nigeria, 1960–61, where he wrote

Echoes from Ibadan (privately published). Since returning to Malawi, where he became Head of the Department of English, he has moved to Botswana.

Mpondo, Simon: b. 1955 in east Cameroon. Sometime lecturer at the College Libermann, Douala. Several of his poems have appeared in *Présence Africaine*.

Mtshali, Oswald: b. 1940 in Natal, South Africa. Worked in various menial capacities. His first book of poems, *Sounds of a Cowhide Drum*, published in 1971 by Renoster Books, made a profound impression as one of the first manifestations of the new angry, energetic and biting voices of black South Africa.

Mugo, Micere Githae: b. in Central Province, Kenya, and studied in Canada. While teaching at Nairobi University, she was detained and held without trial. Upon her release, she moved into exile in Zimbabwe. Joint author with Ngugi wa Thiong'o of the celebrated play *The Trial of Dedan Kimathi*, she has also published a volume of poems, banned in Kenya, *Daughters of My People, Sing* (Kenya Literature Bureau, 1976) and *Visions of Africa* (1978).

Nangolo, Mvula ya: b. in Namibia, Nangolo spent twenty-six years in exile from 1963 onwards, working for the liberation movement SWAPO and broadcasting 'The Voice of Namibia' programme from Dar es Salaam. Upon return to Namibia after independence in 1989, he co-founded *Namibia Today* and continued as a broadcaster. *Thoughts from Exile* was published by Longman Namibia in 1991.

Ndu, Pol N: b. 1940 in Eastern Nigeria. Studied at Nsukka and University of New York. Several of his poems appeared in *Black Orpheus* and *Okike* and his first collection, *Songs for Seers*, was published by Nok in 1974. Tragically killed in a traffic accident in 1978, shortly after his return to Nigeria.

Neto, Augustinho: b. 1922 in Icolo e Bengo region of Angola, his parents being school teachers and Methodists. After secondary-school studies, worked in the colonial health services 1944–7, before going to Coimbra University, Portugal, to study medicine. First arrested 1951 for three months and again in 1952 for joining the Portuguese Movement for Democratic Youth Unity. Arrested again in 1955, he was held till 1957, when, in response to great public pressure, he was released to complete his medical studies. Returned to Angola in 1959 to practise medicine and to lead the underground MPLA. Arrested again in 1960, he was held in Cape Verde Islands and Portugal, whence he escaped in 1962 to assume leadership of the armed struggle against colonial rule. At Angolan independence in 1975 he became President and held the post till his death in 1979. Publications include *Poemas* (Lisbon, 1961) and *Sagrada Esperanca* (Lisbon, 1974; trans. *Sacred Hope*, Dar es Salaam, 1974).

Nokan, Charles: b. 1937 at Yamoussoukro, Côte d'Ivoire, he has published regularly in *Présence Africaine*.

Nortje, Arthur: b. 1942, in Cape Province, South Africa. Attended government high school for coloureds and taught until 1965, when he went to Jesus College, Oxford, to read English. He was briefly imprisoned before leaving South Africa. After teaching in Canada, he returned to Oxford for a higher degree, but took his own life in 1970. His poetry first appeared in *Black Orpheus* in 1961 and he was awarded an Mbari Poetry Prize. His poems were edited and published posthumously by Heinemann as *Dead Roots*, 1973.

Ntiru, Richard: b. 1946 near Kisoro, Uganda. Edited a campus newspaper at Makerere University and contributed to *Zuka* and other journals.

Ofeimun, Odia: b. 1950 in Mid-Western Nigeria. Studied at Ibadan, where he published frequently in *Opon Ifa*, the Ibadan Poetry Chapbooks edited by Femi Osofisan. Took up political service in 1979. His first collection, *The Poet Lied*, was published by Longman in 1980.

Ogundipe-Leslie, Molara: b. 1941 in Western Nigeria. Studied at Ibadan University where she taught for several years before moving to Canada.

Okai, Atukwei: b. 1941 at Accra, Ghana. Took an MA at Gorky Literary Institute, Moscow and an M.Phil. in London before returning to Ghana to lecture in Russian at the university. He became President of the Ghana Association of Writers and gave many public readings of his poetry, of which he has published four volumes to date.

Okara, Gabriel: b. 1921 beside the River Nun in the Niger Delta. After secondary schooling he trained as a binder and worked in the Government Printery at Enugu, where he began to write plays and poetry for radio. Was the first Nigerian poet to appear in *Black Orpheus* (1957). For several years before, during and after the civil war, he served in information and was the first editor of the *Nigerian Tide* newspaper. His collected poems, *The Fisherman's Invocation*, were published by Heinemann in 1978. His only novel, *The Voice*, appeared in 1964.

Okigbo, Christopher: b. 1932 at Ojoto, in Eastern Nigeria. Educated at Government College, Umuahia, and University College, Ibadan, where he read Classics. Employed variously in the civil service, teaching, librarianship (at University of Nigeria, Nsukka) and publishing, he joined the Biafran army in 1967 and died in one of the first battles of the civil war near Nsukka, in September 1967. His poetic cycles *Heavensgate* (1960–62), *Limits* (1962) and *Distances* (1964) were first published in *Black Orpheus* or *Transition* and later by Mbari. The poems he wished to preserve were edited by Okigbo shortly before his death and published by Heinemann as *Labyrinths* in 1971, with his late sequence, *Path of Thunder*, added. Okigbo's fastidiousness as a poet and the urgency of his lyrical voice have exercised a great – perhaps too great an – influence on some younger Nigerian poets, who find it difficult to escape from his shadow.

Ologoudou, Emile: b. 1935 in Ouidah, Benin. Studied law and sociology at University of Dakar 1957–60, then moved to University of Cologne 1960–66. Many of his poems have appeared in *Présence Africaine*.

Osundare, Niyi: b. 1947 in Ikere-Ekiti, Ondo State, Nigeria. Studied at Ibadan, Leeds and Toronto. Contributes frequently to *Opon Ifa* and *West Africa*. Lectures in English at Ibadan University, where he has also written several plays. A frequent contributor to *West Africa*, his witty and elegant *Selected Poems* were published by Heinemann in 1992, winning him the Noma award.

p'Bitek, Okot: b. 1931 in Gulu, Northern Uganda. Educated at Gulu High School and King's College, Budo, where he wrote and produced an opera. Whilst teaching near Gulu, he played football for Uganda and wrote a novel in Lwo, *Lak Tar Miyo Kinyero Wi Lobo* (If your Teeth are White, Laugh!) in 1953. Later studied law in Aberystwyth and social anthropology in Oxford, where he completed a B.Litt. thesis on the traditional songs of Acoli and Lango. Returning to Uganda he worked for some years in extra-mural studies, founding both the Gulu and Kisumu Arts Festivals. *The Song of Lawino* was first composed in Lwo in rhyming couplets and was translated into English in 1966. The Lwo original was also published in 1971. It was followed by *Song of Ocol* (1970) and *Two Songs* (1971), all published by East African Publishing House. He also published a collection of Acoli traditional songs, *The Horn of My Love* (1974), and of Acoli folk-tales, *Hare and Hornbill* (1978). Okot's vigorous and direct poetry exercised an enormous influence throughout Africa. He spent the Amin years in exile and died in 1982, after returning to Uganda.

Peters, Lenrie: b. 1932 in Bathurst (now Banjul) in Gambia. Educated in Freetown and Cambridge, where he read medicine. Well-known as a singer and broadcaster. His first volume of poems was published by Mbari in 1964. In the same year, Heinemann published his novel *The Second Round*. His later volumes, both published by Heinemann, are *Satellites* (1967) and *Katchikali* (1971). Now practises as a surgeon in Banjul.

Rabéarivelo, Jean-Joseph: b. 1901 in Antananarivo, Madagascar, of an impoverished noble family. Left school at thirteen and began writing poetry influenced by the French Symbolists. Founded a literary review and led the literary revival which swept Madagascar in the 1920s and 1930s. Several of his poems appeared in Senghor's anthology in 1948. Passionate and restless in temperament, he drifted from one job to another. He became a drug addict and killed himself in 1937, his despair exacerbated by the refusal of the French authorities to let him travel to France. He published *La Coupe des cendres* (1924), *Sylves* (1927), *Volumes* (1928) and *Presques-songes* (1934). An English translation of some of his works, *24 Songs*, was published by Mbari in 1963 and Heinemann issued *Translations from the Night* a few years later.

Ranaivo, Flavien: b. 1914 in Imerina, near Antananarivo, Madagascar, his father being Governor of Arivonimamo. Did not go to school until he was eight and learnt to read music before the alphabet. Since early childhood has spent much time wandering through the countryside, studying its music, his poetry being much influenced by popular song and ballad forms, especially that called *hain-teny*. His example was important in rooting the new Francophone poetry of Madagascar more deeply in its indigenous poetry and song. Several of his poems appeared in Senghor's anthology. Has published *L'Ombre et le vent* (1947) and *Mes chansons de toujours* (1955).

Rebelo, Jorge: b. 1940 in Lourenzo Marques (now Maputo), Mozambique. Lawyer and journalist, he joined FRELIMO and became its Director of Information during the war of liberation. His poems appeared in *Breve Antologia de Literatura Moçambicana*, published by FRELIMO in 1967.

Rocha, Jofre: b. 1941 in Cachimane near Luanda, Angola. Arriving in Lisbon to study in 1961, he was arrested at the airport and held there and in Luanda until 1963. Joined MPLA and was soon rearrested, being held until 1968. At independence in 1975, became Director-General of External Relations and then Deputy Minister in the same department. In 1978 he became Minister of External Trade. Has published *Tempo do Cicio* (Lobito, 1973), *Estórias de Musseque* (Luanda, 1977) and *Assim se fez Madrugada* (Luanda, 1977).

Rubadiri, James David: b. 1930 in central Malawi. Studied at Makerere College in Uganda, was arrested in the Nyasaland crisis of 1959 but went to Cambridge after his release and read English. Was ambassador in Washington and New York until 1965, when he returned to Makerere and moved later to Nairobi as a university lecturer. His first novel, *No Bride Price*, was published in Nairobi in 1967. Many of his poems have appeared in *Transition*. After the removal of Hastings Banda from power, Rubadiri returned to the Washington embassy.

Rungano, Kristina: b. 1963 in Zimbabwe, she studied Computer Sciences in Britain and now works at the Science Computing Centre in Harare. Her collection *A Storm is Brewing* was published by Zimbabwe Publishing House in 1984.

Sall, Thierno Seydou: b. in Senegal, he published a collection of Wolof poetry with facing French translations in 1991, *Silmaxa* (Paris, Éditions de la Francographie).

Sallah, Tijan: b. 1958 in Gambia and has spent several years studying and teaching in the USA, where he published *Dreams of Dusty Roads* with Three Continents Press in 1992.

Santo, Alda do Espirito: b. 1926 in São Tomé, where she taught for many years. Her poems have appeared in Andrade's anthology and in many Portuguese reviews.

Senghor, Léopold Sédar: b. 1906 in Joal, Senegal, his father being a groundnut merchant and a Roman Catholic in a predominantly Muslim land. Senghor passed brilliantly through the *lycée* in Dakar and went to the Lycée Louis le Grand in Paris in 1928. Later he completed his *agrégation* at the Sorbonne, the first West African to do so. In Paris he met Césaire and Damas with whom he formulated the movement of black cultural assertion known as *négritude*. Before independence, he was variously a Deputy for Senegal in the French National Assembly, a Minister in the French government and a member of the Council of Europe. In 1960 he became the first President of Senegal, holding that post until his retirement in 1981. Throughout his long career in politics, Senghor retained his immense prestige as a pioneer in the reassertion of African cultural values and as the doyen of African poets in French. His style emerged fully formed in his first book, filled with the sombre melody of his long lines and his favourite imagery of the night and the moon, of tender and protective spiritual presences. All his major volumes of poetry have been published by Éditions du Seuil in Paris and include *Chants d'ombres* (1945), *Hosties noires* (1948), *Éthiopiques* (1956) and *Nocturnes* (1961). His collected poems were issued by the same publishers in 1964.

Sepamla, Sipho: b.1932 in Johannesburg, where he has lived all his life. Was editor of the magazine *New Classic*, which has published much of the new South African black poetry. His own volumes include *Hurry up to it!* (1975), *The Blues is You in Me* (1976) and *The Soweto I Love* (1977). Sepamla now runs a dancing academy in Johannesburg.

Serote, Mongane Wally: b.1944 in Sophiatown, Johannesburg, and has spent most of his life in that city. Imprisoned for nine months in 1970, Serote later left for Columbia University on a Fulbright Scholarship and took an MA degree in Fine Arts. Serote then spent several years in exile in London and Botswana, before returning to South Africa to head the ANC's Department of Arts and Culture. His early poems appeared in *The Classic* and in *Purple Renoster*, and Renoster Books brought out his first volume *Yakhal'inkomo* in 1972. A prolific poet, he has recently published *A Tough Tale* (London, Kliptown Books, 1987) and two volumes with David Philip in Johannesburg, *Third World Express* (1992) and *Come and Hope with Me* (1995). His first novel, *To Every Birth Its Blood*, was published by Heinemann in 1981. Serote won the Noma Award in 1993.

Seyaseya, Hopewell: b. in Zimbabwe; published *Counterpoint* jointly with Albert Chimedza in 1984.

Silveira, Onésimo: b.1936 in Cape Verde Islands. Lived for some years in São Tomé and Angola. Joined the liberation movement of Cape Verde and Guinea, the PAIGC, and became its representative in Sweden. His first collection was entitled *Hora Grande*.

Soyinka, Wole: b.1934 in Abeokuta, Western Nigeria. Studied at Government College, Ibadan, University College, Ibadan, and at Leeds University. Taught for a while in London and worked at Royal Court Theatre, which presented an evening of his theatrical sketches and songs. His first plays, *The Swamp Dwellers* and *The Lion and the Jewel*, were produced in London in 1959. In 1960 he returned to Nigeria and threw himself into a period of intense activity as writer, actor and producer. Although chiefly known as Africa's leading dramatist, Soyinka has achieved considerable prominence as a novelist, essayist, poet and teacher (he has headed Theatre Arts Departments at both Ibadan and Ife universities). His early poems appeared in *Black Orpheus* in

1959. In 1967 he published *Idanre & Other Poems*. A small collection, *Poems from Prison*, was published by Rex Collings during his imprisonment in Northern Nigeria 1967–9, and a major collection of poems written then appeared as *A Shuttle in the Crypt* in 1972. A long narrative poem, *Ogun Abibiman*, was published by Opon Ifa in 1976 and by Rex Collings in 1977. Soyinka also edited *Transition/Ch'indaba* in Accra 1973–6. Soyinka was awarded the Nobel Prize for Literature in 1986. Late in 1994 he left Nigeria secretly after the confiscation of his passport by the military government and is now living in exile.

Tati-Loutard, Jean-Baptiste: b. 1939 in Ngoyo, Congo Republic. Educated at Pointe Noire, Brazzaville and Bordeaux, where he studied Modern Literature and Italian, writing a thesis on Benedetto Croce. Whilst in France, published his first two volumes of poetry, *Poèmes de la mer* (Yaoundé, 1968) and *Les Racines congolaises* (P. J. Oswald, 1968). His later volumes include *L'Envers du soleil* (P. J. Oswald, 1970) and *Les Normes du temps* (Lubumbashi, 1974). After teaching at the University of Brazzaville, he joined the Nguesso government as Minister of Culture. Despite a busy public life as a minister, he continued to pour out poetry of exceptional intensity. Like the late Tchicaya U Tam'si, he sings of the rivers, forests and ocean strands of the Congo. Recent volumes include *Les Feux de la planète* (1977), *La Tradition du songe* (1985) and *Le Serpent austral* (1992), the last two with Présence Africaine, who also published his prose memoir *Le Récit de la mort* (1987). He has won many awards, including a gold medal from the Académie française in 1992.

Tidjani-Cissé, Ahmed: b. 1947 in Conakry, Guinea. Left Guinea in 1963 and studied law and political science in Paris, where he is a professor of African Dance and director of an African ballet troupe. Has recently published a play, *Maudit soit Cham*, with Éditions Nubia, which also published his poems, *Pollens et fleurs*, in 1980. The latter won the prize Poésie Plurielle in 1981.

U Tam'si, Tchicaya: b. 1931 in Mpili, Congo Republic. In 1946 accompanied his father, then Deputy for Congo, to France and studied in Orléans and Paris. In addition to his many volumes of poetry, he wrote many radio features, plays and stories. His first novel, *Les Concrélats*, was published by Albin Michel in 1980 and a collection of stories, *La Main sèche*, by Juillard in the same year. Apart from a short spell in Kinshasa as editor of a newspaper during the Lumumba era, Tchicaya lived in France from his childhood, but his work with UNESCO enabled him to visit the African continent frequently. His first volume, *Le Mauvais sang*, was published in 1955 and was reissued with *Feu de brousse* and *À triche-coeur* by P. J. Oswald in 1970. Oswald also reissued *L'Arc musical* and *Épitomé* in the same year. In 1978 Tchicaya published *La Veste d'intérieur* with Éditions Nubia, and an expanded edition of *Le Ventre* with Présence Africaine. An English translation of *Feu de brousse* was published by Mbari in 1964, whilst Gerald Moore's *Selected Poems of Tchicaya U Tam'si*, published by Heinemann in 1970, contains the whole of *À triche-coeur* and *Épitomé*, together with selections from *Le Ventre* and *L'Arc musical*. Undoubtedly the major francophone poet of his generation, U Tam'si died suddenly in Paris in 1988.

Wendel, Ngudia: b. 1940 in Icolo e Bengo region, near Luanda, Angola. Has spent his whole adult life with MPLA, first as a guerrilla leader and later, after training in the Soviet Union, as a doctor. In 1973–4 was Director of Medical Services on the Northern Front and in Cabinda. His collection *Nos Volteramos, Luanda!* (We Shall Return, Luanda!) was published in Lusaka in 1970 and in a bilingual Portuguese–Italian edition at Forli in 1974.

Wonodi, Okogbule: b. 1936 in Port Harcourt, Eastern Nigeria. After training as a teacher, studied and taught at Nsukka. Later attended the Writers' Workshop at Iowa University. Under the military regime in Nigeria of 1975–9 he was for some years Chairman of Port Harcourt Town Council. His first volume, *Ucheke*, was published by Mbari in 1964 and he contributed frequently to *Black Orpheus*.

Yambo, Ouologuem: b. 1940 in the Dogon country of Mali Republic, only son of a school inspector. Went to Paris in 1962 to study philosophy, literature and sociology. His first novel, *Le Devoir de violence*, won the Prix Renaudot in 1968. This was followed by the vigorous satirical pamphlet, *Lettre ouverte à la France-nègre*, addressed to General de Gaulle. His poetry has not been collected, but several poems appeared in *Nouvelle somme*.

Zimunya, Musaemura Bonas: b. in Mutare, Zimbabwe, and grew up in Eastern Highlands. Lectures at University of Zimbabwe and has published *Kingfisher, Jikinya and Other Poems* (Longman Zimbabwe, 1982).

Sources of the Poems

N.B. The following works are frequently referred to below and marked *q.v.* for ease of reference

(i) *African Women's Poetry*, ed. Frank and Stella Chipasula (London, Heinemann, 1995).

(ii) Andrade, Mario de, *Antologia de la poesia negra de espressão portuguesa* (Lisbon, 1953, reissued by P. J. Oswald, Honfleur, 1969).

(iii) *Black Orpheus*, founded and edited by Ulli Beier, published in Ibadan twice yearly 1957–67. Second series, edited by J. P. Clark and Abiola Irele, appeared at intervals from 1968 onwards.

(iv) *Nouvelle somme de poésie du monde noir*, ed. Paolin Joachim, *Présence Africaine* (Paris, No. 57, 1966).

(v) *Poems from Angola*, ed. and trans. Michael Wolfers (London, Heinemann, 1979).

(vi) *Poems of Black Africa*, ed. Wole Soyinka (London, Heinemann, 1975).

(vii) *Présence Africaine*, founded by the late Alioune Diop, published thrice yearly in Paris since 1947. The oldest journal of African literature and culture, it is an archive of extraordinary value. The publishing house of the same name is one of the main publishers of African theatre, fiction and poetry.

(viii) *Reflections*, ed. Frances Ademola (Lagos, African Universities Press, 1962).

(ix) *Transition*, founded and edited by Rajat Neogy, published thrice yearly in Kampala 1961–8 and in Accra 1971–6. Wole Soyinka became editor in 1973 and the last two issues were retitled *Ch'indaba*.

(x) *When Bullets Begin to Flower*, ed. and trans. Margaret Dickinson (Nairobi, East African Publishing House, 1972).

(xi) *Zuka*, literary journal published occasionally in Nairobi.

(xii) *Okike*, founded and first edited by Chinua Achebe in 1971. Soon moved its editorial offices from Amherst, Massachusetts, to Nsukka, Nigeria.

(xiii) *West Africa*, published weekly in London for many decades. Originally a commercial and political journal, it has in recent years become more African-oriented in editorial policy and readership; an important organ for the publication of African poetry in English.

Aidoo: from *African Women's Poetry, q.v.*

Aig-Imoukhuede: from MS.

Aiyejina: from MS.

Amadiume: from *Passion Waves* (London, Karnak Press, 1986).

Andrade: from *Poems from Angola, q.v.*

Anyidoho: 'Hero and Thief' from *West Africa*, 14 June 1982; 'Soul in Birth-waters' from *A Harvest of Our Dreams* (Heinemann, 1984); rest from *Earthchild* (Accra, Woeli Publications, 1985).

Armah: from *West Africa*, 23 May 1983 (copyright © A. K. Armah).

Asalache: from MS.

Awoonor: 'Songs of Sorrow', 'Song of War', and 'The Sea Eats the Land at Home' from *Okyeame*, 1 (Accra, 1961); 'Lovers' Song', 'The Weaver Bird' and 'Easter Dawn' from *Rediscovery* (Ibadan, Mbari Publications, 1964); 'At the Gates' from *Night of My Blood* (Doubleday, 1971); 'Afro-American Beats' from *Ride Me, Memory* (New York, Greenfield Review Press, 1973); 'The First Circle' from *The House by the Sea* (New York, Greenfield Review Press, 1978); 'Had Death Not Had Me in Tears' from *Until the Morning After: Collected Poems* (New York, Greenfield Review Press, 1987).

Ba: from *Paroles plaisantes au coeur et à l'oreille* (la Pensée Universelle, 1977).

Bognini: 'My Days Overgrown' (trans. Ulli Beier) from *Black Orpheus*, 18, 1965; 'Earth and Sky' from *Ce dur appel de l'espoir* (Présence Africaine, 1960). Other poems (trans. Gerald Moore) from *Herbe féconde* (P. J. Oswald, 1973).

Bolamba: from *Esanzo* (Présence Africaine, 1956): trans. Gerald Moore.

Brew: from *Okyeame*, 1 (Accra, 1961).

Brutus: first three poems from *Sirens, Knuckles, Boots* (Ibadan, Mbari Publications, 1963); 'Poems About Prison: 1' from *A Simple Lust* (Heinemann, 1973).

Cheney-Coker: first six poems from *The Graveyard Also Has Teeth* (Heinemann, 1980); 'The Philosopher' from MS; 'The Tin Gods' and 'The Brotherhood of Man' from *The Blood in the Desert's Eyes* (Heinemann, 1990).

Chimedza: from *Counterpoint* (Harare, College Press, 1984).

Chimombo: both from *Napolo and the Python* (Heinemann, 1994).

Chipasula, Frank: 'A Love Poem for My Country', 'The Witch Doctor's Song' and 'A Hanging' from *O Earth, Wait for Me* (Johannesburg, Ravan Press, 1984); 'Nightfall' and 'Nightmare' from *Whispers in the Wings* (Heinemann, 1991); 'Blantyre' and 'The Rain Storm' from MS.

Chipasula, Stella: from *African Women's Poetry, q.v.*

Clark: first five poems from *Poems* (Ibadan, Mbari Publications, 1962); 'A Child Asleep' from *Black Orpheus*, 13, 1963; 'The Leader' from *A Reed in the Tide* (Longman, 1965); 'Season of Omens' from *Casualties* (Longman, 1970).

Craveirinha: from Andrade's anthology, *q.v.*

d'Erneville: from *African Women's Poetry, q.v.*: trans. Brian Baer.

de Sousa: 'Appeal' from Andrade's anthology, *q.v.*; 'If You Want to Know Me' (trans. Art Brakel) from *Ba Shiru* (Madison, Wisconsin, Spring 1970).

Diop, Birago: all poems from *Leurres et lueurs* (Présence Africaine, 1960): trans. Gerald Moore and Ulli Beier.

Diop, David: all poems from *Coups de pilon* (Présence Africaine, 1956): trans. Gerald Moore and Ulli Beier.

Dipoko: 'Pain' and revised version of 'Exile' from MS. 'Our Life' from *Transition*, Vol. 4, No. 10, 1963; other poems from *Black and White in Love* (Heinemann, 1972).

Dongala: from *Nouvelle somme*, *q.v.*: trans. Gerald Moore.

Echeruo: 'Melting Pot' from *Black Orpheus*, 12 (Ibadan, 1963); 'Man and God Distinguished' from *Mortality* (Longman, 1968).

Fatoba: all poems from *Petals of Thought* (London, New Beacon Books, 1984).

Gashe: from *African Women's Poetry*, *q.v.*

Higo: 'Ritual Murder' from *Transition*, Vol. 3, No. 8, 1963; 'Hidesong' from *Transition*, Vol. 3. No. 9, 1963.

Jacinto: 'Monangamba' from Andrade's anthology, *q.v.*; other poems from *Poems from Angola*, *q.v.*

Jemie: from *Voyage* (Ife, Papua Pocket Poets, 1971).

Kadima-Nzuji: from *Présence Africaine*, 97, 1976: trans. Gerald Moore.

Kalimbukwha: from MS.

Kariara: from *Zuka*, 1, Nairobi.

Kayo: 'Song of the Initiate' from *Nouvelle somme*, *q.v.*; 'War' from *Paroles intimes* (P. J. Oswald, 1972): both trans. Gerald Moore.

Kgositsile: 'The Air I Hear' from MS; 'Song for Ilva Mackay and Mongane' from *Transition/Ch'indaba*, 2, 1976; 'The Present is a Dangerous Place to Live' from *Okike*, 3 (Amherst, Massachusetts, 1972); 'When the Deal Goes Down' and 'Montage: Bouctou Lives' from *To the Bitter End* (Chicago, Third World Press, 1995).

Komey: 'The Change' from *Black Orpheus*, 9, 1961; 'Oblivion' from *Messages*, ed. Awoonor and Adali-Morty (Heinemann, 1971).

Konie: from *African Women's Poetry*, *q.v.*

Kunene: 'The Echoes' and 'Elegy' from MS; 'Thought on June 26' from *Poems of Black Africa*, *q.v.*

Laing: all poems from *Godhorse* (Heinemann, 1989).

Maina: from *Season of Blood* (London, Vita Books, 1995).

Makisosila: From *Chants polyphoniques des pogroms de Luanda* (Paris, Éditions Racines et Couleurs, 1995): trans. Gerald Moore.

Malangatana: from *Black Orpheus*: trans. Dorothy Guedes.

Mapanje: first six poems from *Of Chameleons and Gods* (Heinemann, 1981); rest from *The Chattering Magpies of Mikuyu Prison* (Heinemann, 1993).

Marechera: from *West Africa*, 6 September 1982; and *Cemetery of Mind* (Harare, Baobab Books, 1992).

Massaki: from *Chants polyphoniques des pogroms de Luanda* (Paris, Éditions Racines et Couleurs, 1995): trans. Gerald Moore.

Mattera: all poems from *Azanian Love Song* (Johannesburg, Skotaville Books, 1983).

Maunick: from *Les Manèges de la mer* (Présence Africaine, 1964): trans. Gerald Moore.

Mhlophe: from *African Women's Poetry*, *q.v.*

Mnthali: from *Echoes from Ibadan* (Ibadan, privately printed, 1961).

Mpondo: from *Présence Africaine*, 93, 1975.

Mtshali: from *Sounds of a Cowhide Drum* (Johannesburg, Renoster Books, 1971).

Mugo: from *African Women's Poetry*, *q.v.*

Nangolo: from *Thoughts from Exile* (Windhoek, Longman Namibia, 1991).

Ndu: 'udude' from *Black Orpheus*, 18, 1965; 'Evacuation' from *Songs for Seers* (Nok Publications, 1974).

Neto: 'Farewell at the Moment of Parting' (trans. Gerald Moore) from Andrade's anthology, *q.v.*; 'African Poem' and 'Kinaxixi' (trans. W. S. Merwin) from *Black Orpheus*, 15, 1964; 'The Grieved Lands of Africa' from *Poems from Angola*, *q.v.*

Nokan: from *Nouvelle somme*, *q.v.*: trans. Gerald Moore.

Nortje: from MS.

Ntiru: from *Poems of Black Africa*, *q.v.*

Ofeimun: first three poems from *The Poet Lied* (Longman, 1980); 'Break Me Out' from *West Africa*, 15 March 1982.

Ogundipe-Leslie: from *Okike*, 21, 1982.

Okai: from *Poems of Black Africa*, *q.v.*

Okara: 'The Snowflakes Sail Gently Down' from *Reflections*, *q.v.*; rest from *The Fisherman's Invocation* (Heinemann, 1978).

Okigbo: first six poems from *Heavensgate* (Ibadan, Mbari Publications, 1962); next four poems from *Limits* (Ibadan, Mbari Publications, 1964); two movements of *Distances* from *Transition*, Vol. 4, No. 16, 1964; rest from *Labyrinths* (Heinemann, 1971).

Okri: from *An African Elegy* (Jonathan Cape, 1992).

Ologoudou: from *Nouvelle somme*, *q.v.*: trans. Gerald Moore.

Osundare: first two poems from *I Sing of Change* (Ibadan, privately printed, 1981); rest from *Selected Poems* (Heinemann, 1992).

p'Bitek: from *The Song of Lawino* (Nairobi, East African Publishing House, 1966) and from *The Song of Prisoner* in *Two Songs* (Nairobi, East African Publishing House, 1970).

Peters: 'Homecoming', from *Black Orpheus*, 11, 1962; 'One Long Jump' and 'Parachute Men' from *Poems* (Ibadan, Mbari Publications, 1964); 'Isatou Died' from *Katchikali* (Heinemann, 1971).

Rabéarivelo: all poems from Senghor's anthology; English translations by Ulli Beier and Gerald Moore from *24 Poems* (Ibadan, Mbari Publications, 1963).

Ranaivo: poems from Senghor's anthology, *q.v.*: trans. Gerald Moore.

Rebelo: 'Poem' from *When Bullets Begin to Flower*, *q.v.*; 'Poem for a Militant' (trans. Art Brakel) from *Ba Shiru* (Madison, Wisconsin, Spring 1970).

Rocha: from *Poems from Angola*, *q.v.*

Rubadiri: from MS.

Rungano: from *African Women's Poetry*, *q.v.*

Sall: from *Silmaxa* (Paris, Éditions de la Francographie, 1991): trans. Gerald Moore.

Sallah: from *Dreams of Dusty Roads* (Washington, Three Continents Press, 1992).

Santo: 'Where are the Men Seized in This Wind of Madness?' from Andrade's anthology, *q.v.*: trans. Gerald Moore; 'Grandma Mariana': trans. Julia Kirst from *African Women's Poetry*, *q.v.*.

Senghor: all poems from *Poèmes* (Paris, Éditions du Seuil, 1964): trans. Gerald Moore and Ulli Beier.

Sepamla: all poems from *The Soweto I Love* (Rex Collings, 1977).

Serote: first three poems from *Poets to the People*, ed. Barry Feinberg (Allen & Unwin, 1974); extract from *Come and Hope with Me* (Johannesburg, David Philip, 1995).

Seyaseya: from *Counterpoint* (Harare, College Press, 1984).

Silveira: from *When Bullets Begin to Flower*, *q.v.*

Soyinka: 'Death in the Dawn' and 'Abiku' from *Black Orpheus*, 10, 1962; 'Massacre, October '66' and 'Civilian and Soldier' from *Idanre* (Eyre Methuen, 1967); 'Prisoner' from *Reflections*, *q.v.*; 'Season' from *Encounter*; 'Night' from MS; 'Ujamaa', 'Amber Wall', 'I Anoint my Flesh' and 'Hanging Day: Procession' from *A Shuttle in the Crypt* (Eyre Methuen, 1972).

Tati-Loutard: 'News of My Mother' from MS; 'The Voices', 'Submarine Tombs' and 'Pilgrimage to Loango Strand', from *Poèmes de la mer* (Yaoundé, Éditions Cléa, 1968); 'Noonday in Immaturity' and 'Death and Rebirth' from *Les Racines congolaises* (P. J. Oswald, 1968); 'Secret Destiny' from *La Tradition du songe* (Paris, Présence Africaine, 1985); 'End of Flight' and 'Letter to Edouard Maunick' from *Le Serpent austral* (Paris, Présence Africane, 1992): all poems trans. Gerald Moore.

Tidjani-Cissé: from *Pollens et fleurs* (Éditions Nubia, 1980): trans. Gerald Moore.

U Tam'si: 'Brush-fire', 'Dance to the Amulets' and 'A Mat to Weave' from *Brushfire* (Ibadan, Mbari Publications, 1964): trans. Ulli Beier; all other poems from *Selected Poems* (Heinemann, 1970): trans. Gerald Moore.

Veiga: from *African Women's Poetry*, *q.v.*: trans. Julia Kirst.

Wendel: from *Poems from Angola*, *q.v.*

Wonodi: 'Planting' from *Ucheke* (Ibadan, Mbari Publications, 1964); 'Salute to Icheke' from *Black Orpheus*, 19, 1966.

Yambo: from *Nouvelle somme*, *q.v.*: trans. Gerald Moore.

Zimunya: from *Kingfisher, Jikinya and Other Poems* (Harare, Longman Zimbabwe, 1982).

Acknowledgements

For permission to publish or republish the poems in the anthology, acknowledgement is made to the poets and to the following copyright holders:

For Ama Ata Aidoo to Heinemann Educational Publishing; for Funso Aiyejina to the author; for Ifi Amadiume to Karnak Press; for Costa Andrade to Heinemann Educational Publishing; for Kofi Anyidoho to *West Africa*, Greenfield Review Press and Woeli Publications; for Ayi Kwei Armah to the author; for Kofi Awoonor to the author, Mbari Publications, *Okyeame*, Doubleday & Co. and Greenfield Review Press; for Oumar Ba to la Pensée Universelle; for Joseph Miezan Bognini to Présence Africaine and P. J. Oswald; for Antoine-Roger Bolamba to Présence Africaine; for Kwesi Brew to *Okyeame*; for Dennis Brutus to Mbari Publications and Heinemann Educational Publishing; for Syl Cheney-Coker to Heinemann Educational Publishing; for Albert Chimedza to College Press; for Steve Chimombo to Heinemann Educational Publishing; for Frank Chipasula to the author and Ravan Press; for Stella Chipasula to the author; for J. P. Clark to Mbari Publications, *Black Orpheus* and Longman; for José Craveirinha to P. J. Oswald; for Annette M'Baye d'Erneville to Heinemann Educational Publishing; for Noémia de Sousa to P. J. Oswald and *Ba Shiru*; for Birago Diop to Présence Africaine; for David Diop to Présence Africaine; for Mbella Sonne Dipoko to *Transition* and Heinemann Educational Publishing; for Emmanuel Dongala to Présence Africaine; for Michael Echeruo to *Black Orpheus* and Longman; for Femi Fatoba to New Beacon Books; for Marina Gashe to Heinemann Educational Publishing; for Aig Higo to *Transition*; for Antonio Jacinto to P. J. Oswald and Heinemann Educational Publishing; for Onwuchekwa Jemie to Papua Pocket Poets; for Lemuel Johnson to the author; for Mukula Kadima-Nzuji to Présence Africaine; for Albert Kalimbakatha to the author; for Amadou Elimane Kane to Editions Nouvelles du Sud; for Jonathan Kariara to *Zuka*; for Patrice Kayo to Présence Africaine and P. J. Oswald; for Keorapetse Kgositsile to *Transition/Ch'indaba*, *Okike* and Third World Press; for Ellis Ayitey Komey to *Black Orpheus* and Heinemann Educational Publishing; for Gwendoline Konie to Heinemann Educational Publishing; for Mazisi Kunene to Heinemann Educational Publishing; for Kojo Laing to Heinemann Educational Publishing; for Maina wa Kinyatti to Vita Books; for Mawete Makisosila to Editions Racines et Couleurs; for Valente Malangatana to *Black Orpheus*; for Jack Mapanje to Heinemann Educational Publishing; for Dambudzo Marechera to *West Africa* and Academic and Baobab Books; for Makuzayi Massaki to Editions Racines et Couleurs; for Don Mattera to Skotaville Books; for Edouard Maunick to Présence Africaine; for Gcina Mhlophe to the author; for Simon Mpondo to Présence Africaine; for Oswald Mtshali to Renoster Books; for Micere Githae Mugo to Heinemann Educational Publishing; for Mvula ya Nangolo to the author; for Pol N Ndu to *Black Orpheus* and Nok Publications; for Augustinho Neto to P. J. Oswald, *Black Orpheus* and Heinemann Educational Publishing; for Charles Nokan to Présence Africaine; for Richard Ntiru to the author; for Odia Ofeimun to Longman and *West Africa*; for Molara Ogundipe-Leslie to *Okike*; for Atukwei Okai to Heinemann Educational Publishing; for Gabriel Okara to African Universities Press, *Black Orpheus* and Heinemann Educational Publishing; for Christopher Okigbo to Mbari Publications, *Transition* and Heinemann Educational Publishing; for Ben Okri to the author c/o David Godwin Associates and Jonathan Cape Ltd; for Emile Ologoudou to Heinemann Educational Publishing; for Niyi Osundare to Heinemann Educational Publishing; for Okot p'Bitek to East African Publishing House; for Lenrie Peters to *Black Orpheus*, Mbari Publications and Heinemann Educational Publishing; for Jean-Joseph Rabéarivelo and Flavien Ranaivo to Presses Universitaires de la France; for Jorge Rebelo to East African Publishing House and *Ba Shiru*; for Jofre Rocha to Heinemann Educational Publishing; for Kristina Rungano to Heinemann Educational Publishing; for Seydou Sall to Editions de la Francographie; for Tijan Sallah to Lynne Rienner Publishers; for Barolong Seboni to the author; for Alda do Espirito Santo to P. J. Oswald; for Léopold Sédar Senghor to Editions de Seuil and *Black Orpheus*; for Sipho Sepamla to Rex Collings; for Mongane Wally Serote to George Allen & Unwin and David Philip Publishers; for Hopewell Seyaseya to College Press; for Onésimo Silveira to East African Publishing House; for Wole Soyinka to Leavy, Rosensweig & Hyman on behalf of the author, *Black Orpheus*, Eyre Methuen Ltd, African Universities Press and *Encounter*; for Jean-Baptiste Tati-Loutard to Editions Cléa, P. J. Oswald and Présence Africaine; for Ahmed Tidjani-Cissé to Nubia; for Tchicaya U Tam'si to Caractères, P. J. Oswald, *Black Orpheus* and Heinemann Educational Publishing; for Amélia Veiga to Heinemann Educational Publishing; for Ngudia Wendel to Heinemann Educational Publishing; for Okogbule Wonodi to *Black Orpheus* and *Transition*; for Ouologuem Yambo to Présence Africaine; for Musaemura Bonas Zimunya to Longman Zimbabwe Ltd.

Every effort has been made to contact or obtain permission from all copyright holders whose work is newly published in this volume, but in some cases this has not proved possible. The publishers would be pleased to make any corrections or rectify any omissions brought to their attention at the earliest opportunity.

Index of Poets

Index of First Lines

READ MORE IN PENGUIN

In every corner of the world, on every subject under the sun, Penguin represents quality and variety – the very best in publishing today.

For complete information about books available from Penguin – including Puffins, Penguin Classics and Arkana – and how to order them, write to us at the appropriate address below. Please note that for copyright reasons the selection of books varies from country to country.

In the United Kingdom: Please write to *Dept. EP, Penguin Books Ltd, Bath Road, Harmondsworth, West Drayton, Middlesex UB7 ODA*

In the United States: Please write to *Consumer Sales, Penguin Putnam Inc., P.O. Box 999, Dept. 17109, Bergenfield, New Jersey 07621-0120.* VISA and MasterCard holders call 1-800-253-6476 to order Penguin titles

In Canada: Please write to *Penguin Books Canada Ltd, 10 Alcorn Avenue, Suite 300, Toronto, Ontario M4V 3B2*

In Australia: Please write to *Penguin Books Australia Ltd, P.O. Box 257, Ringwood, Victoria 3134*

In New Zealand: Please write to *Penguin Books (NZ) Ltd, Private Bag 102902, North Shore Mail Centre, Auckland 10*

In India: Please write to *Penguin Books India Pvt Ltd, 210 Chiranjiv Tower, 43 Nehru Place, New Delhi 110 019*

In the Netherlands: Please write to *Penguin Books Netherlands bv, Postbus 3507, NL-1001 AH Amsterdam*

In Germany: Please write to *Penguin Books Deutschland GmbH, Metzlerstrasse 26, 60594 Frankfurt am Main*

In Spain: Please write to *Penguin Books S. A., Bravo Murillo 19, 1° B, 28015 Madrid*

In Italy: Please write to *Penguin Italia s.r.l., Via Benedetto Croce 2, 20094 Corsico, Milano*

In France: Please write to *Penguin France, Le Carré Wilson, 62 rue Benjamin Baillaud, 31500 Toulouse*

In Japan: Please write to *Penguin Books Japan Ltd, Kaneko Building, 2-3-25 Koraku, Bunkyo-Ku, Tokyo 112*

In South Africa: Please write to *Penguin Books South Africa (Pty) Ltd, Private Bag X14, Parkview, 2122 Johannesburg*

READ MORE IN PENGUIN

Penguin Twentieth-Century Classics offer a selection of the finest works of literature published this century. Spanning the globe from Argentina to America, from France to India, the masters of prose and poetry are represented by the Penguin.

If you would like a catalogue of the Twentieth-Century Classics library, please write to:

Penguin Marketing, 27 Wrights Lane, London W8 5TZ

(Available while stocks last)

READ MORE IN PENGUIN

A CHOICE OF TWENTIETH-CENTURY CLASSICS

Orlando Virginia Woolf

Sliding in and out of three centuries, and slipping between genders, Orlando is the sparkling incarnation of the personality of Vita Sackville-West as Virginia Woolf saw it.

Selected Poems Patrick Kavanagh

One of the major figures in the modern Irish poetic canon, Patrick Kavanagh (1904–67) was a post-colonial poet who released Anglo-Irish verse from its prolonged obsession with history, ethnicity and national politics. His poetry, written in an uninhibited vernacular style, focused on the 'common and banal' aspects of contemporary life.

More Die of Heartbreak Saul Bellow

'One turns the last pages of *More Die of Heartbreak* feeling that no image has been left unexplored by a mind not only at constant work but standing outside itself, mercilessly examining the workings, tracking the leading issues of our times and the composite man in an age of hybrids' – *New York Book Review*

Tell Me How Long the Train's Been Gone James Baldwin

Leo Proudhammer, a successful Broadway actor, is recovering from a near-fatal heart attack. Talent, luck and ambition have brought him a long way from the Harlem ghetto of his childhood. With Barbara, a white woman who has the courage to love the wrong man, and Christopher, a charismatic black revolutionary, Leo faces a turning-point in his life.

Memories of a Catholic Girlhood Mary McCarthy

Blending memories and family myths, Mary McCarthy takes us back to the twenties, when she was orphaned in a world of relations as colourful, potent and mysterious as the Catholic religion. 'Superb ... so heartbreaking that in comparison Jane Eyre seems to have got off lightly' – Anita Brookner

READ MORE IN PENGUIN

A SELECTION OF POETRY

American Verse
British Poetry since 1945
Caribbean Verse in English
Chinese Love Poetry
A Choice of Comic and Curious Verse
Contemporary American Poetry
Contemporary British Poetry
Contemporary Irish Poetry
English Poetry 1918–60
English Romantic Verse
English Verse
First World War Poetry
German Verse
Greek Verse
Homosexual Verse
Imagist Poetry
Irish Verse
Japanese Verse
The Metaphysical Poets
Modern African Poetry
New Poetry
Poetry of the Thirties
Scottish Verse
Surrealist Poetry in English
Spanish Verse
Victorian Verse
Women Poets
Zen Poetry